Ask a Question
LIFE ON EARTH

ARMADILLO

This paperback edition printed in 2009

© 1997 Bookmart Limited

ISBN: 978-1-84322-714-4

1 3 5 7 9 10 8 6 4 2

Published by Armadillo Books, an imprint of
Bookmart Limited, Registered Number 2372865
Trading as Bookmart Limited, Blaby Road,
Wigston, Leicestershire, LE18 4SE, England

Text: Nicola Baxter
Design: Amanda Hawkes
Cover Design: Anthony Prudente
Editorial Consultant: Ronne Randall

Originally published in 1998 as part of
1000 Questions & Answers

Printed in Thailand

CONTENTS

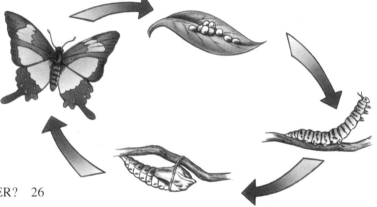

WHERE IN THE UNIVERSE ARE WE?

The universe is the name we give to all of space. Astronomers use huge telescopes, both on Earth and in space, to measure light, x-rays and radio waves from objects that are billions of light years away. Earth is one of the nine planets that orbit our Sun. It is part of the Milky Way Galaxy, one of billions of galaxies in the universe.

Sun　　Mars　　Saturn　　Venus　　Neptune

Mercury　　Earth　　Jupiter　　Uranus　　Pluto

WHICH IS THE NEAREST STAR?

THE SUN is our nearest star. It is 149.6 million km (92.9 million miles) away from Earth. Stars are massive nuclear reactors, generating energy in their cores. It is the heat and light from the Sun that makes life on Earth possible. The huge gravity pull of the Sun keeps the planets of our Solar System orbiting around it.

WHAT ARE THE PLANETS OF THE SOLAR SYSTEM?

THE FIRST FOUR planets are known as the Inner Planets. The remaining five are the Outer Planets.

Planet	Diameter	Length of year	No. of moons
Mercury	4878km	88 Earth days	0
Venus	12,103km	225 Earth days	0
Earth	12,756km	365 Earth days	1
Mars	6794km	687 Earth days	2
Jupiter	142,800km	11.9 Earth years	16
Saturn	120,000km	29.5 Earth years	18
Uranus	52,400km	84.0 Earth years	15
Neptune	49,400km	164.8 Earth years	8
Pluto	1100km	248.5 Earth years	1

WHAT IS A GALAXY?

A GALAXY is an enormous group of stars held together by gravity. Our galaxy, the Milky Way, is in the shape of a spiral. Other galaxies are elliptical or irregular. There may be 100 billion galaxies in the universe. Many of them are grouped together in clusters, with huge areas of space in between.

spiral galaxy   elliptical galaxy   irregular galaxy

WHY DO CONSTELLATIONS HAVE SUCH STRANGE NAMES?

HUMAN BEINGS have always tried to see pictures in the patterns the stars make. The names given to those pictures by European scholars in medieval times and earlier are often used by astronomers today. Most of them are in Latin as that was the language of scholarship in Europe for hundreds of years.

Aquila (the eagle)

Scorpius (the scorpion)

fast facts

IS THERE LIFE ELSEWHERE IN THE UNIVERSE?

As there are so many billions of planets in the universe, it may be that life exists on some of them. In 1996 scientists believed they had discovered signs of fossilized life in a meteorite that landed on Earth from Mars.

WHAT ARE SHOOTING STARS?

Shooting stars are meteors, made of particles of rock and dust, that shine brightly as they burn up in the Earth's upper atmosphere.

WHY IS IT SOMETIMES HARD TO SEE THE STARS?

The stars are still there! It may be that cloud is covering the night sky. Also, there is so much artificial light at night now, from homes and street lighting, that it is often not dark enough to see the stars.

WHAT IS AN ECLIPSE?

Eclipses happen for a brief period when the Moon, Earth and Sun are in line. A lunar eclipse happens when the Earth lies between the Moon and the Sun, blocking off the light to the Moon, so that the Moon seems to vanish. A solar eclipse is when the Moon blocks the Sun's light from the Earth, so that the Sun seems to disappear.

Space travel gave human beings their first opportunity to see the Earth from outside the Earth's atmosphere.

WHEN DID SPACE EXPLORATION BEGIN?

THE FIRST ARTIFICIAL SATELLITE, *Sputnik 1*, was launched by the USSR in October 1957. The same year, a dog called Laika was the first living creature to travel in space in *Sputnik 2*. It was the USSR again that put the first human in space in 1961, when Yuri Gagarin travelled in *Vostok 1*. In 1969, US astronauts were the first to land on the Moon in *Apollo 11*.

As there is no wind or weather on the Moon to erase them, the footprints left by astronauts are still there!

WHY DOES THE MOON CHANGE SHAPE EACH MONTH?

OF COURSE, the Moon does not really change shape – it just seems as though it does. The Moon orbits the Earth once every 27.3 days. It has no light of its own, but as it moves around, it is lit by the Sun. Only the part of the Moon that is both turned towards the Earth and lit by the Sun is visible on Earth. The amount of the Moon's surface that can be seen changes as the Moon's position changes.

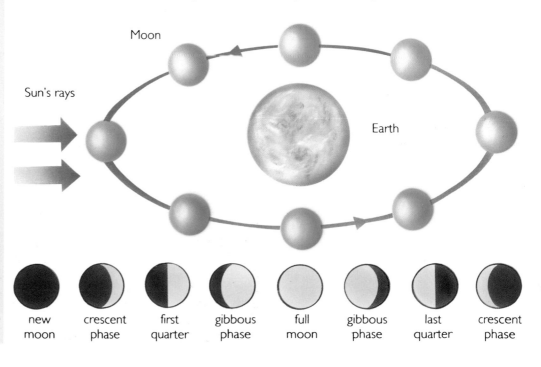

Moon

Sun's rays

Earth

new moon | crescent phase | first quarter | gibbous phase | full moon | gibbous phase | last quarter | crescent phase

WHAT IS INSIDE THE EARTH?

Beneath the land and water that cover the Earth's surface lie layers of rock and metal at very high temperatures. The deepest mines ever dug have not reached the bottom of the outer layer, called the crust. Under the crust, a layer called the mantle is thought to be made partly of solid and partly of molten rock. At the centre of the Earth, there is an outer core of molten metal and an inner core of solid metal, probably largely iron.

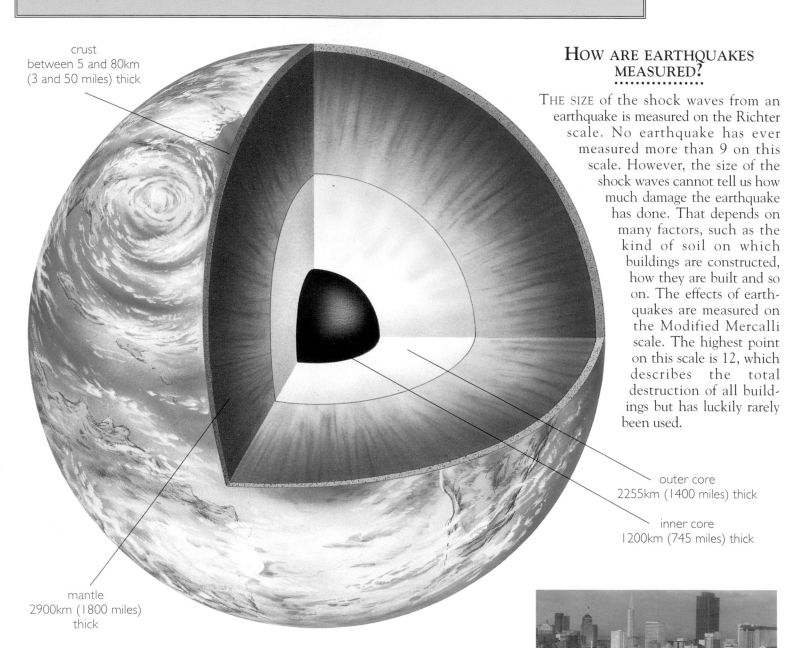

crust
between 5 and 80km
(3 and 50 miles) thick

mantle
2900km (1800 miles)
thick

outer core
2255km (1400 miles) thick

inner core
1200km (745 miles) thick

HOW ARE EARTHQUAKES MEASURED?

THE SIZE of the shock waves from an earthquake is measured on the Richter scale. No earthquake has ever measured more than 9 on this scale. However, the size of the shock waves cannot tell us how much damage the earthquake has done. That depends on many factors, such as the kind of soil on which buildings are constructed, how they are built and so on. The effects of earthquakes are measured on the Modified Mercalli scale. The highest point on this scale is 12, which describes the total destruction of all buildings but has luckily rarely been used.

WHAT CAUSES EARTHQUAKES?

THE EARTH'S CRUST is made up of 15 pieces or "plates", which float on the molten rock below. The places where these plates meet are called faults. Along the lines of faults, the plates move and push against each other. Sometimes this causes a violent shock, with waves of tremors moving out and shaking the Earth's surface.

The San Andreas fault runs along the west coast of the United States of America. Most older houses in San Francisco, which lies near the fault, are built of wood. They do not collapse as easily as brick buildings if the ground shakes.

CAN ANY BUILDING WITHSTAND AN EARTHQUAKE?

NO STRUCTURE can withstand very large earthquakes, but by using reinforced materials and foundations that allow for movement, architects have been able to design buildings able to survive even quite strong shocks.

In Tokyo new buildings are designed to withstand most earth tremors.

WHAT IS A GEYSER?

IN SOME AREAS, underground lakes, rivers and springs are heated by molten rocks below. The hot water bubbles to the surface in springs and forms pools, or it may shoot upwards under great pressure, forming a geyser.

This famous geyser in Yellowstone National Park, USA, is known as "Old Faithful".

WHY DO VOLCANOES ERUPT?

LIKE EARTHQUAKES, volcanoes mainly occur along fault lines. Molten rock, gases and ash are forced out through a gap in the Earth's crust to release the pressure beneath. Over thousands of years, cooled rock sometimes builds up around the fissure in the ground to form the familiar conical shape of a volcano.

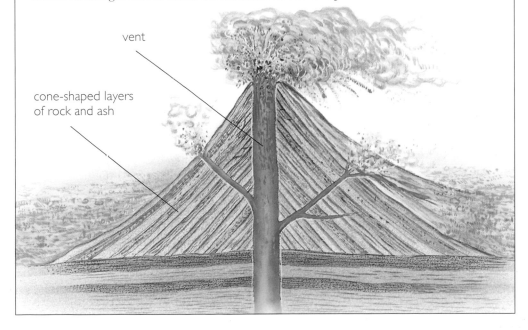

vent

cone-shaped layers of rock and ash

WHAT CAN VOLCANOES TELL US?

ONE interesting aspect of volcanic eruptions is that surrounding areas are covered rapidly in molten rock or ash, sometimes preserving the animals, plants and structures underneath. Archaeologists have been able to study life in Roman times, for example, by examining the remains of Pompeii, in Italy, buried when Vesuvius erupted in AD 79.

fast facts

CAN EARTHQUAKES BE PREDICTED?

Not very well. Scientific instruments attempt to detect early signs, and the behaviour of birds and animals may give warning of a shock, but none of these methods is currently foolproof.

WHAT IS THE EPICENTRE OF AN EARTHQUAKE?

The epicentre is the point on the Earth's surface directly above where the earthquake occurs. Shock waves move out from the epicentre to surrounding areas.

WHAT IS A TSUNAMI?

A tsunami is a huge tidal wave, caused by an undersea earthquake. It is dangerous to shipping and can also cause damage on land when it breaks over the coast.

ARE THERE VOLCANOES UNDER THE SEA?

Most active volcanoes *are* under the sea! Their effects are usually not noticed on land.

WHAT IS A DORMANT VOLCANO?

Dormant means "sleeping". A dormant volcano might erupt in the future. An *extinct* volcano, on the other hand, will not become active again.

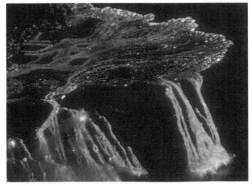

The lava flow from a volcano can be spectacular, as this photograph of Kilauea Volcano, Hawaii, shows.

WHEN DID LIFE BEGIN ON EARTH?

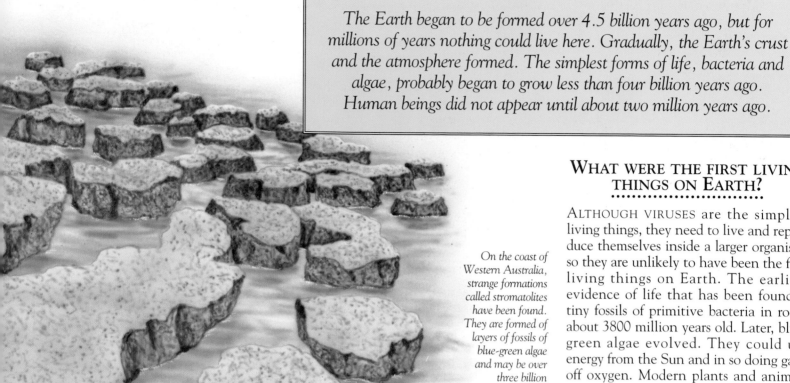

The Earth began to be formed over 4.5 billion years ago, but for millions of years nothing could live here. Gradually, the Earth's crust and the atmosphere formed. The simplest forms of life, bacteria and algae, probably began to grow less than four billion years ago. Human beings did not appear until about two million years ago.

On the coast of Western Australia, strange formations called stromatolites have been found. They are formed of layers of fossils of blue-green algae and may be over three billion years old.

WHAT WERE THE FIRST LIVING THINGS ON EARTH?

ALTHOUGH VIRUSES are the simplest living things, they need to live and reproduce themselves inside a larger organism, so they are unlikely to have been the first living things on Earth. The earliest evidence of life that has been found is tiny fossils of primitive bacteria in rocks about 3800 million years old. Later, blue-green algae evolved. They could use energy from the Sun and in so doing gave off oxygen. Modern plants and animals share these simple organisms as ancestors.

HOW DO WE KNOW ABOUT PREHISTORY?

ALMOST EVERYTHING that we know about the living things on Earth before humans evolved has been learnt from fossils. Fossils are the remains of dead animals and plants that have been turned to stone over millions of years.

An animal dies and is covered by sediment washed on top of it.

Under great pressure, the sediment slowly solidifies into rock.

Minerals fill the space left by the body or bones and also become rock.

Over thousands of years, weather and the Earth's movement may bring the fossil to the surface.

HOW ARE PREHISTORIC TIMES DESCRIBED?

THE PERIODS when the Earth was forming and early kinds of life were developing have been given names. There is also a short way of saying "55 million years ago": 55mya.

WHEN DID THE EARTH BEGIN TO LOOK AS IT DOES TODAY ?

THE SURFACE of the Earth is changing all the time. When living things first began to evolve on Earth, there was just one huge continent. Over millions of years, this continent broke up and moved to become the land masses we recognize today. This is why similar dinosaur fossils have been found in very different parts of the world, although dinosaurs were land creatures and could not cross the oceans.

PRECAMBRIAN 4600–590mya	PALEOZOIC 590–248mya						MESOZOIC 248–65mya		
	Cambrian	Ordovician	Silurian	Devonian	Carboniferous	Permian	Triassic	Jurassic	Cretaceou

fast facts

WHAT IS PREHISTORY?

Prehistory is what we call the time before written records.

CAN WE SEE EVOLUTION HAPPENING?

It takes many, many generations for evolutionary changes to take place, so we cannot usually see them happening. But as some insects live for a day or less, scientists can trace changes in them in only a few years.

WHAT IS PALAEONTOLOGY?

Palaeontology is simply the scientific name for the study of fossils.

ARE NEW FOSSILS STILL BEING FOUND?

Every year fossils are found that add to our knowledge of prehistoric life. Very often they are discovered by ordinary people walking in the countryside. Places where soil is frequently being washed away from rocks, such as at the bottom of cliffs, are good places to look.

WHAT IS EVOLUTION?

LIVING THINGS inherit characteristics from the generations that have gone before, but each individual is slightly different. Over many generations, the differences that are more successful survive, so that the species gradually adapts. In time, these changes, called evolution, can lead to major adaptations and even new species. All living things have evolved from the simple organisms that began to grow in the Earth's waters. Many of these, such as the dinosaurs, have since become extinct, although they may have lived successfully on Earth for millions of years.

WHEN WERE FOSSILS DISCOVERED?

EVER SINCE HUMAN BEINGS first lived on Earth they have been finding fossilized remains. But it was really only in the nineteenth century that scientific study of the fossils took place. Until then, people believed that the fossils came from dragons, giants or even unicorns!

There are large gaps in the fossil record that have puzzled scientists. That is why there was once talk of "missing links" – living things that had evolved to a point between early fossil forms and modern creatures and plants. Although some modern reptiles look as ancient as dinosaurs, they are not directly descended from them, but they may share a common ancestor.

250 million years ago, there was one giant continent, now named Pangaea.

LAURASIA   GONDWANALAND

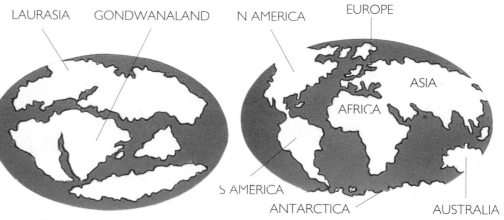

135 million years ago, Pangaea had split into two main continents: Laurasia and Gondwanaland.

N AMERICA   EUROPE   ASIA   AFRICA   S AMERICA   ANTARCTICA   AUSTRALIA

As millions of years passed, the continents we know today began to form.

CENOZOIC
65mya–today

Tertiary   Quaternary

DID DINOSAURS RULE THE EARTH?

During the 150 million years that they lived on Earth, dinosaurs certainly included the largest creatures to live on land and the fiercest hunters. But they were not the only animals to live successfully on Earth by any means. There were many species of insect and the earliest winged animals could be seen in the skies. The seas were teeming with fish and other sea-life. The first mammals were also thriving, ready to become the dominant creatures when the dinosaurs became extinct.

WHAT COLOUR WERE DINOSAURS?

DINOSAUR FOSSILS, even when they show the skin of the animal, cannot show us what colour it was. Dinosaurs may have been green and brown in colour, camouflaging them amongst the leaves and rocks. It is also possible that some of them were very brightly coloured, just as some tropical lizards are today.

This scene shows what the landscape may have looked like during the Cretaceous period. In many parts of the world there were plentiful streams and rivers, with marshy plains in between. Lush vegetation allowed the plant-eating dinosaurs to grow even larger.

Iguanodon was a plant-eater, tearing leaves from high branches.

Baryonyx had sharp claws and teeth. It is likely that it ate fish from streams and lakes.

Polacanthus was a plant-eating dinosaur, browsing near the ground. Its spines helped to protect it from attack.

Fossil footprints show that some dinosaurs, such as *Hypsilophodon*, seem to have moved in groups. As with herds of browsing animals today, this meant that they were safer from predators.

ARE FOSSILS THE ONLY EVIDENCE OF LIFE IN PREHISTORIC TIMES?

OVER TIME, the remains of plants and animals decay. Fossilization is one way in which their forms have survived to give us information about prehistoric times. Since the time of the dinosaurs, however, the climate of parts of the Earth has cooled. In recent years, frozen remains of mammoths and even humans have been found, preserved in the ice of polar or mountainous regions.

Another source of information about prehistoric life is cave painting. In several parts of the world, early paintings have been found on rocks, often hidden from view for thousands of years. Viewed by the flickering light of torches, as they would have been when first painted, the animals almost seem to move.

WHAT HAPPENED TO THE DINOSAURS?

ONE THEORY is that climate changes gradually led to a drop in dinosaur numbers. Another is that a huge meteorite hit the Earth, throwing up a massive dust cloud. Mammals managed to survive the climate change, but dinosaurs did not.

WHO WERE THE FIRST HUMANS?

SCIENTISTS believe that humans and apes had a common ancestor. About five million years ago in Africa, some hominids (early humans) began to walk on two legs. Over millions of years, they developed bigger brains and began to spread out to other parts of the world. Later hominids began to make tools, develop language, use fire and wear clothes. The scientific name for modern people is *Homo sapiens sapiens*. They invented farming about 9000 years ago. Their early settlements led to the first civilizations.

Homo habilis made stone tools.

Homo erectus used fire and could live in cooler climates.

Homo sapiens neanderthalensis lived in Europe and had burial ceremonies.

Homo sapiens sapiens, modern man, does not seem to have evolved from Homo sapiens neanderthalensis.

fast facts

DID DINOSAURS HAVE COLD BLOOD?

Like modern reptiles, dinosaurs were probably cold-blooded creatures, although this is difficult to prove. Some dinosaurs may have had "sails" on their backs to help them to regulate their body heat.

HOW MANY KINDS OF DINOSAUR WERE THERE?

Fossils of over 350 different species of dinosaur have been discovered, but it is likely that there were many more than this. There are certainly many more fossils of all kinds waiting to be found.

DID DINOSAURS ATTACK HUMANS?

Dinosaurs became extinct about 65 million years ago, over 60 million years before humans lived on Earth.

WHICH WERE THE LARGEST DINOSAURS?

The plant-eating *sauropods* were the largest dinosaurs. They are the biggest land animals ever to have lived on Earth. Some were over 30m (100ft) long.

WERE DINOSAURS CLEVER?

Dinosaurs were very successful – they lived on Earth for over 150 million years – but as far as we know they all had quite small brains. *Stegosaurus'* brain was only 5cm (2 inches) long.

DID DINOSAURS CARE FOR THEIR YOUNG?

It used to be thought that dinosaurs laid their eggs and left them to hatch, as turtles do. Discoveries of the fossils of young dinosaurs with adult members nearby now suggest that some dinosaurs did care for their young, perhaps even sitting on the eggs to hatch them.

HOW ARE LIVING THINGS CLASSIFIED?

Living things are classified in groups that have certain characteristics in common. The largest groups are called kingdoms. All living things can be classified as belonging to one of the five kingdoms: animals, plants, fungi, protists and monerans. Kingdoms can be divided into phyla (singular: phylum) or divisions and subphyla, which in turn can be separated into classes. Classes are divided into orders and suborders. These are separated into families and then into genera (singular: genus). Finally, each genus contains a number of species.

WHICH ARE THE SIMPLEST LIVING THINGS?

MEMBERS of the moneran and protist families are the simplest organisms. Individuals are much too small to be seen without a microscope.

HOW IS A LION CLASSIFIED?

LIONS belong to the:

Animal (*Animalia*) kingdom
Chordate (*Chordata*) phylum
Mammal (*Mammalia*) class
Carnivore (*Carnivora*) order
Cat (*Felidae*) family
Big cat (*Panthera*) genus
Lion (*leo*) species

The scientific name for lions is *Panthera leo*, the last two divisions.

WHICH IS THE LARGEST GROUP OF LIVING THINGS?

THE CLASS of insects is the largest class of living things, containing over one million different species.

WHY DO LIVING THINGS HAVE LATIN NAMES?

THE SYSTEM of classifying living things was invented by a Swedish botanist called Carolus Linnaeus (1707–78). Latin was traditionally the language used by scholars, so the classifications have Latin names. This also means that living things can be identified by scientists in every country, no matter what the local name for a species might be.

Classifying millions of living things is very complicated. This chart has been simplified to include the main groups of plants and animals.

KEY

KINGDOM

phylum

class

MONERANS

single-celled organisms without a cell nucleus, such as bacteria

PROTISTS

single-celled organisms with a cell nucleus, such as amoebas and diatoms

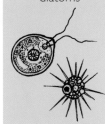

FUNGI

organisms with bodies made of a mass of threads, feeding on plants and animals, such as moulds, mildews and mushrooms

PLANTS

have cell walls of cellulose, and most make their food from sunlight by photosynthesis

mosses

ferns

ANIMALS

can move for at least part of their lives, feeding on plant or animal matter

sponges

molluscs

sea anemones, jellyfish, corals

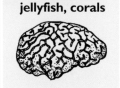

flatworms, tapeworms

star fish, sea urchins

roundworms

leeches, worms

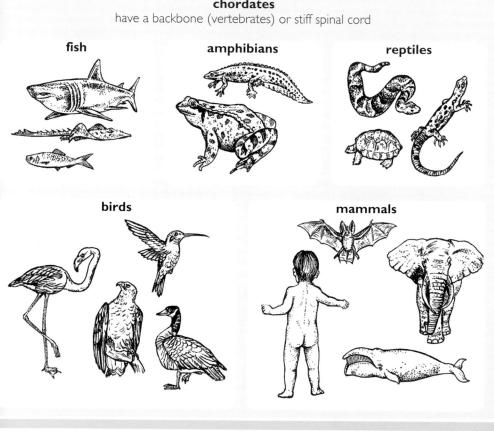

conifers

flowering plants

monocotyledons
have seeds with only
one seed-leaf
(cotyledon)

dicotyledons
have seeds with two seed-leaves

chordates
have a backbone (vertebrates) or stiff spinal cord

fish

amphibians

reptiles

birds

mammals

arthropods
have jointed bodies, divided into segments, with an external skeleton

horseshoe crabs

millipedes

centipedes

scorpions, spiders

insects

crabs, lobsters, shrimps

fast facts

ARE NEW SPECIES STILL BEING DISCOVERED?

There are many parts of the Earth where new species are still being discovered, including the rain-forests, which are teeming with living things, and the oceans, still the least explored part of our planet.

HOW ARE NEW SPECIES NAMED?

Usually new species can be fitted into an existing genus. The species name may describe a characteristic of the new discovery or show where it was found, or it may be named after the person who found it.

WHAT IS AN EXTINCT SPECIES?

An extinct species is one where there are no more living examples on Earth.

HOW MANY SPECIES HAVE BECOME EXTINCT?

Species are evolving all the time. The climate, new predators, or the success of other species may cause them to become extinct. It is thought that as many as 95% of the species that have ever lived on Earth are now extinct.

DOES THE CLASSIFICATION OF LIVING THINGS EVER CHANGE?

When Linnaeus first proposed his system of classification, he based his decisions mainly on the appearance of the living things. Since then, scientists have been able to study the physical and chemical structures of organisms and form views on how they evolved historically. This has meant that some living things have been reclassified as more is known about them.

HOW DO PLANTS LIVE?

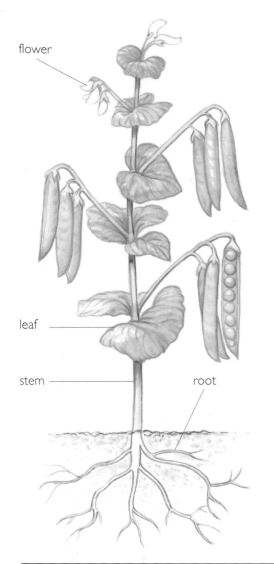

flower

leaf

stem

root

Like animals, plants need food for energy to survive and grow, but while animals can move about to catch their food or find new areas of vegetation, plants are usually rooted to one spot. But plants can do something that no animal can do. They can make energy from sunlight. This process is called photosynthesis. As well as light, plants also need water and nutrients.

HOW DOES PHOTOSYNTHESIS WORK?

A PLANT'S LEAVES contain a green substance called chlorophyll. The chlorophyll enables chemical reactions to take place. These use energy from the Sun and carbon dioxide gas from the air to make food for the plant to live and grow. As photosynthesis happens, oxygen is given off into the air.

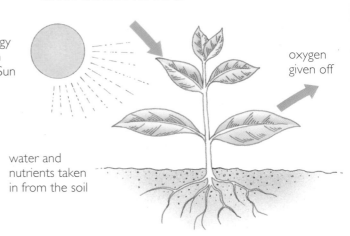

carbon dioxide from the air

light energy from the Sun

oxygen given off

water and nutrients taken in from the soil

WHAT ARE PLANTS USED FOR APART FROM FOOD?

OVER THOUSANDS OF YEARS, human beings have found many uses for plants. Some of the most common ones are shown here.

Both linen and cotton threads, used to make fabric, come from plants.

Most paper is made from the cellulose fibres found in wood pulp.

Rubber comes from the sap of a tropical tree.

Sisal and hemp are tough plant fibres used for ropes and matting.

Many objects, including buildings, are made from wood.

Plant extracts are used in perfumes and many cosmetic and cleaning preparations.

WHY ARE PLANTS IMPORTANT?

IF THERE WERE NO PLANTS, there could not be animal life on Earth. All animals either eat plants or eat other animals that in turn eat plants themselves. In this way, every living thing on Earth indirectly gets its energy from the Sun, although only plants can convert the Sun's light into a usable form.

Humans use milk and meat from cows for energy. Cows take in energy from plants. Plants convert energy from the Sun. This is called a food chain.

HOW DO PLANTS REPRODUCE?

THERE ARE TWO MAIN WAYS in which plants reproduce. In sexual reproduction, pollen is transferred by insects or the wind from one part of a flower to another, in such a way that fertilization can take place. Seeds are then formed. These seeds in turn are distributed in different ways to a spot where they can germinate and grow.

Seeds may be surrounded by fleshy fruit. Some fruits, such as cherries, contain just one seed. Others, like this papaya, have many seeds inside.

This popular houseplant produces small plants at the end of stems. If put in soil, these will grow and can be separated from the parent plant.

In asexual reproduction, a plant can reproduce without fertilization taking place. It may, for example, reproduce by sending out runners from its roots or by growing new plants on the tips of its leaves or branches.

DO PLANTS REALLY EAT INSECTS?

SOME PLANTS do gain extra minerals and other nutrients by trapping and "eating" insects. They are usually found in areas where there are not enough nutrients in the soil for healthy growth.

When an insect lands on tiny hairs on the Venus' flytrap's sensitive leaf tips, the pairs of leaves snap shut, trapping the insect inside.

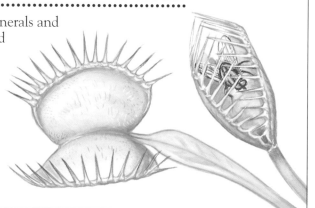

HOW HAVE HUMANS CHANGED PLANTS?

ABOUT 9000 years ago, human beings invented farming. Since then, they have carefully selected the crops that give the best harvests under different conditions. Particularly in the last two hundred years, selective plant breeding has developed the characteristics that farmers and consumers require. Now that machines are used to pick most crops, and large stores prefer to package fruits and vegetables in regular sizes, many commercial varieties have been bred to produce even fruits that ripen together.

In the wild, flowers appear over a period of weeks. Commercial growers have bred varieties that will flower and can be picked all at one time.

fast facts

WHAT IS A WEED?

A weed is simply a plant that is growing somewhere inconvenient for a gardener or farmer.

WHAT IS A PARASITIC PLANT?

A parasitic plant does not grow in the soil but on another plant. It does not photosynthesize but takes the food it needs through its roots or stem from its host plant.

CAN PLANTS FEEL?

Although plants do not have feelings in the way that we do, they can certainly respond to different stimuli. They are able to grow towards a light source, even if turned upside down. Some plants have very sensitive leaves, which will fold up if touched.

ARE ALL PLANTS GREEN?

Most plants are green, but a few also have other pigments that mask the green colour. Red seaweed is an example of this kind of plant.

WHICH ARE THE SMALLEST PLANTS?

Green algae are single-celled plants. They form, for example, the greenish film often found on the bark of trees. Millions of cells of the algae are needed to cover the tree trunk.

DO ALL PLANTS HAVE FLOWERS?

Flowering plants are known as angiosperms. Although there are plenty of plants that do not have flowers, such as mosses, ferns, algae and conifers, the majority of plants on Earth are flowering ones. That does not mean that they are what we generally think of as flowers – colourful blooms that can be presented in bouquets. Most trees and grasses, for example, are flowering plants, but their flowers may be so small that they usually go unnoticed.

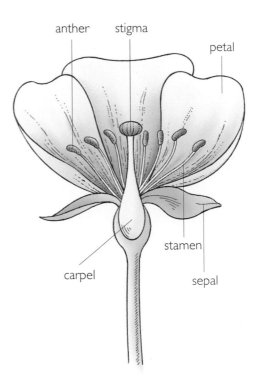

Although many plants have flowers with both male and female parts, as in this cross-section, some have male and female flowers on the same plant, and some have only male or only female flowers. Holly trees are an example of this. In order for a female holly to produce berries, it must be fertilized by a nearby male holly, which will never produce berries.

WHAT ARE FLOWERS FOR?

FLOWERS are the reproductive parts of a plant. Usually, one flower has both male and female parts. The male parts are the stamens, which consist of filaments and anthers. Filaments are like little stalks that support the anthers. Anthers produce tiny dust-like grains called pollen. The female part of a flower is called the carpel. This consists of an ovary, ovules, a style and a stigma. The ovary is hidden in a bulb-shaped receptacle at the base of the flower. Inside the ovary are one or more ovules, which become seeds if the flower is fertilized. Rising from the ovary is a small, sticky stem called the style, the tip of which is the stigma. In order for a flower to be fertilized, pollen must be transferred from the male stamen to the female stigma.

WHY ARE THERE SO MANY FLOWER SHAPES?

THE DIFFERENT SHAPES of flowers help to ensure that they are fertilized. Flowers that rely on insects for pollination must make sure that the insect is carrying pollen from the same kind of plant. The shape of the flower ensures that only certain kinds of insect can pollinate it. Flat flowers, such as daisies and sunflowers, can be visited by hoverflies and some bees. Flowers that are formed into tubes only attract insects that have long tongues. As flowers bloom at different times of the year, there are usually only a few different species available to each insect at any one time, so the chances of pollination are increased.

The ancestors of these garden flowers developed different formations of petals, stamens and carpels. Over the centuries, horticulturists have developed these shapes further by selective breeding.

fast facts

WHICH IS THE LARGEST FLOWER?

The largest flower in the world is *Rafflesia arnoldii*, from Asia. Its flowers can measure over 1m (3ft) across.

WHAT ARE PERENNIALS, BIENNIALS AND ANNUALS?

Some plants grow from a seed, flower, produce their own seeds and die all in one year. They are called annuals. Those taking two years to complete their life cycle are called biennials. Plants that live for several years, even if they die down in the winter, are called perennials.

WHAT IS POT-POURRI?

This fragrant mixture is usually made from dried flower petals, spices and sweet-smelling oils. It was very useful in the days when rooms – and people – were dirtier and smellier than we would like today, but pot-pourri is still popular for its sweet scent.

WHAT IS THE LANGUAGE OF FLOWERS?

From early times, flowers have been thought to have a special meaning when presented to a loved one. The Victorians developed this to a fine art. An admirer sending a red rose to signify "pure love" might receive the reply of a Michaelmas daisy, meaning "farewell"!

HOW HAVE FLOWERS HELPED HISTORIANS?

Flowers seem very delicate, but parts of them last almost indefinitely in the right conditions. This is particularly true of pollen, which can still be recognized long after it was part of a growing plant. Historians have been able to tell which plants grew in ancient times by examining the pollen found in tombs and graves thousands of years old.

HOW ARE FLOWERING PLANTS FERTILIZED?

THE POLLEN that fertilizes the stigma may come from the same flower or from a nearby flower. Many flowers are fertilized (or pollinated) by insects. The flowers produce drops of a sweet liquid called nectar at the base of their petals. When insects visit the flower to drink the nectar, pollen from the anthers rubs off onto their wings, bodies and legs. When the insect visits another flower, the pollen is deposited on its sticky stigma.

Some plants, such as willows and hazels, have long dangling flowers called catkins. The wind is their pollinator, as great clouds of pollen blow off in the breeze and find their way to neighbouring catkins.

HOW ARE SEEDS DISPERSED?

WHEN THE FLOWER has been fertilized, the ovary swells to form a fruit, inside which one or more seeds will grow. These seeds may simply fall to the ground below, or the plant may have methods of ensuring that its offspring grow much further away.

Some seeds in fruits and berries have tough outer cases with fleshy fruits around them. The seeds can pass through the digestive system of birds and grow wherever the birds' droppings fall.

Dandelion seeds are dispersed by the wind. Each seed has a hairy parachute that can carry it for many metres.

Some trees rely on animals to carry their seeds far away. Squirrels, for example, collect acorns and nuts and may bury them to eat later. Often these stores are forgotten, and the seeds grow where they were buried.

HOW ARE NEW FLOWERS BRED?

FLOWERS that are closely related often cross-pollinate in the wild, creating a variety of flower shades and shapes. Under controlled conditions, plant breeders ensure that their parent plants are not pollinated naturally. They then transfer pollen from a selected "father" plant to the stigma of the "mother" plant and wait for seeds to form. These are sown to see what kind of flowers result. It may be years before the results are known and even then only a few of the plants will prove to be different and attractive enough to be launched as new varieties.

WHICH ARE THE BIGGEST PLANTS?

Trees are the largest plants on Earth and play a very important part on the planet. They cover almost a quarter of the Earth, helping to stabilize the atmosphere by taking in huge amounts of carbon dioxide from the air and giving off oxygen. In addition, tree roots help to retain fertile soil and stop the rain from washing it down hillsides, while the huge amount of water vapour given off by trees has an important effect on the weather.

WHY ARE TREES IMPORTANT?

AS WELL AS directly affecting the environment, trees supply homes and food for millions of other living creatures, including people. They are also the source of wood, which is used in buildings and for making such essential items as furniture and paper.

DO TREES HAVE FLOWERS?

TREES can be divided into two groups. Broad-leaved trees, which may also be deciduous, meaning that they drop their leaves in winter, are flowering plants. Sometimes their flowers are very small and difficult to spot. Conifers, most of which are evergreen, retaining their leaves all year round, are cone-bearers. They have small male cones and larger female cones instead of flowers.

apple-tree flowers   cone

The trunk, branches, leaves and roots of this tree provide food and shelter for many insects, birds and animals. Some plants, too, grow on these much larger plants.

HOW ARE YOUNG TREES PRODUCED?

TREES PRODUCE SEEDS just as smaller plants do. Their flowers or cones are fertilized by the wind, or insects or birds. But a parent tree takes up large amounts of water from the area around it, and its leaves prevent sunlight from reaching the ground beneath, so it is important that all the seeds do not fall directly beneath the tree. Some trees produce fruits that are eaten by birds or animals and carried far away in their digestive systems. Others bear seeds that have "wings" and can be blown far away by the wind.

Hawthorn berries pass through the digestive system of birds before the seeds germinate. In winter, birds are glad of fruits to eat, as insects are hard to find.

HOW CAN YOU TELL HOW OLD A TREE IS?

IN TEMPERATE CLIMATES, a tree makes rapid growth in the warm spring and summer months and much slower growth in the autumn and winter. This growth shows in the trunk as a light ring during times of fast growth and a darker ring for slower growth. It is therefore possible to count the pairs of light and dark rings to see how many years the tree has been growing.

Counting the rings of some ancient trees shows that they were growing when the pharaohs ruled Egypt.

HOW CAN YOU IDENTIFY A TREE?

OFTEN the easiest way to identify a deciduous tree is to look at the shape of its leaves. The general shape of the tree, the way in which the branches join and the pattern of the bark also give clues, especially in winter when the leaves have fallen.

fast facts

WHAT IS THE TALLEST TREE IN THE WORLD?

The giant sequoia is not only the tallest tree in the world but the tallest living thing of any kind. It can reach over 90m (270ft).

WHICH TREES LIVE THE LONGEST?

Yew trees can live to a very great age, but the oldest living tree is probably a bristlecone pine, in the western United States, which is over 4300 years old.

HOW MANY SPECIES OF TREE ARE THERE?

There are thought to be about 40,000 species of tree, of which about 700 are conifers.

WHAT WERE THE FIRST TREES LIKE?

Trees have been on Earth longer than many animals. The first trees were cone-bearing.

DO ALL TREES GROW TALL?

The dwarf willow, which grows in the Scottish highlands, reaches only 2.5cm (1 inch) in height.

WHAT IS AN INVERTEBRATE?

The leech has 33 segments in its body.

An invertebrate is an animal without a backbone. More than 90% of all animals are invertebrates. Insects form the largest group of invertebrates. Like millipedes and centipedes, crustaceans and spiders, they are arthropods, with jointed bodies and an outer protective casing. There are also many soft-bodied creatures, such as worms and jellyfish, often living in water or damp areas where sun and air will not dry out their bodies. Molluscs are also soft-bodied, but many of them are protected by an outer shell.

WHICH INVERTEBRATES CAN BE MISTAKEN FOR PLANTS?

CNIDARIANS are invertebrates, mainly living in the sea, that have a single space inside them where food is digested. A mouth leads from the outside to the space, which is called the coelenteron. Often the mouth is surrounded by tentacles, which help to catch food and pass it into the coelenteron. Corals, sea anemones and jellyfish are all cnidarians. Both corals and sea anemones can look like plants at first sight.

Brightly coloured sea anemones look like exotic flowers but are in fact made of jelly. Their waving tentacles have stinging cells to attack any small fish that swims through them. The tentacles then shorten to draw the fish into the body of the anemone, where it is slowly digested.

HOW MANY DIFFERENT KINDS OF WORM ARE THERE?

THERE ARE well over fifty thousand different kinds of worm, divided into three main groups. The annelids have bodies that are divided into segments. They include earthworms and leeches. Roundworms, also known as nematodes, do not have segments. Many of these are crop pests, eating plants and making crops prone to diseases. Others are parasites, living on or in other animals, some causing serious diseases in humans. Finally, flatworms also include several parasites, including some with a complicated life cycle that involves them living in two different animal hosts one after the other.

Tapeworms are flatworms that live and·lay eggs inside an animal. The eggs are passed out in the animal's waste matter and can then infect another host.

The coral reefs to be found in tropical waters are made from millions of little creatures, rather like sea anemones, called polyps. They live in colonies begun by just one polyp that "buds" and produces new polyps. Each polyp builds a hard skeleton around itself. When the polyps die, their skeletons remain.

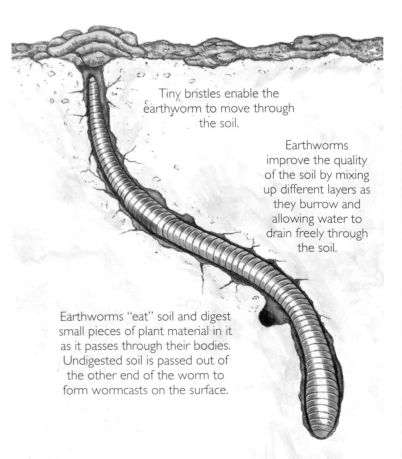

Tiny bristles enable the earthworm to move through the soil.

Earthworms improve the quality of the soil by mixing up different layers as they burrow and allowing water to drain freely through the soil.

Earthworms "eat" soil and digest small pieces of plant material in it as it passes through their bodies. Undigested soil is passed out of the other end of the worm to form wormcasts on the surface.

HOW DOES A MAN O' WAR CATCH ITS FOOD?

ALTHOUGH at first sight the man o' war appears to be a jellyfish, in fact it is made up of a whole colony of polyps, each of which has a particular job to do. Some form stinging tentacles; others digest food; and one large polyp is filled with gas to form the "sail" that allows the man o' war to float, powered by the wind.

WHICH ANIMALS HAVE THEIR SKELETONS ON THE OUTSIDE?

ARTHROPODS have skeletons on the outside, which give them several advantages over soft-bodied animals. The skeleton forms a waterproof casing, preventing the body from drying out and allowing the animal to live outside water or damp places. In addition, skeletons on the outside, just like those on the inside, give muscles a firm anchoring point, so that the animal is often stronger than soft-bodied creatures of a similar size.

Centipedes, millipedes, spiders, insects and crustaceans are all arthropods. Some crustaceans, such as many crabs and lobsters, have particularly hard outer casings. Shrimps and barnacles are also crustaceans.

WHAT IS A MOLLUSC?

AFTER INSECTS, molluscs form the largest group of animals. Molluscs have soft, muscular bodies, often covered by a protective shell. Some, such as snails, move on a muscular foot, which can be withdrawn into the shell for protection. Other, sea-dwelling molluscs, such as squid and scallops, take in water and squirt it out to jet-propel themselves along.

fast facts

DO YOU SHARE YOUR BATH WITH AN INVERTEBRATE?

Sponges are invertebrates! Natural sponges are the bodies of sea-dwelling animals. When alive, the sponge draws water through its holes to trap tiny food particles, which are then absorbed.

HOW HAVE LEECHES BEEN USED BY DOCTORS?

Leeches are segmented worms with a sucker at each end. Some leeches attach themselves to animals and suck their blood. In the past, doctors used leeches to "bleed" a patient, thinking that they could draw out sickness that way. Today scientists are looking at the leech's ability to produce a chemical that stops blood from clotting, to see how this could help human beings.

WHICH IS THE LARGEST INVERTEBRATE?

The largest invertebrate is a mollusc, the giant Atlantic squid (*Archteuthis*), which can reach 20m (66ft).

HOW DO CENTIPEDES AND MILLIPEDES DIFFER?

Centipedes are meat-eaters with only one pair of legs on each body segment. Vegetarian millipedes, however, have two pairs of legs on each segment.

HOW COMMON IS THE COMMON EARTHWORM?

Earthworms live in soil in which there is at least some plant material for them to eat. There can be well over seven million earthworms in every hectare of topsoil (over 17 million per acre).

CAN ALL INSECTS FLY?

Most insects have wings at one time or another in their lives, although a very few species, such as fleas, silverfish, firebrats and springtails, do not. Flying insects have two pairs of wings – forewings and hindwings – although not all of them use both pairs for flying. All insects have a tough outer skeleton, six legs and bodies divided into three distinct parts, but there is enormous variation between insect species.

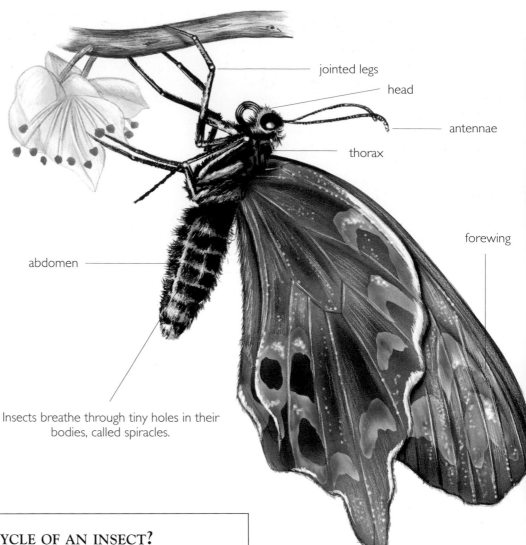

jointed legs

head

antennae

thorax

forewing

abdomen

Insects breathe through tiny holes in their bodies, called spiracles.

hindwing

WHAT IS THE LIFE CYCLE OF AN INSECT?

YOUNG INSECTS develop in two main ways. In some species, such as grasshoppers and locusts, the young that hatch from eggs look rather like small adults, and are called nymphs. As they grow, the nymphs shed their skins, looking more and more like adults each time.

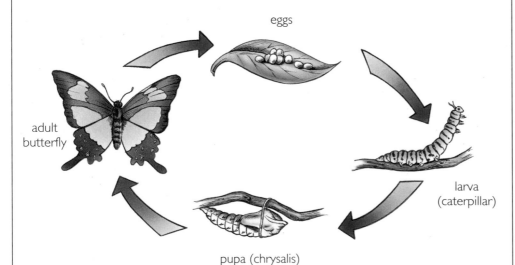

eggs

adult butterfly

larva (caterpillar)

pupa (chrysalis)

Other insects, such as butterflies, bees and beetles, go through a process called metamorphosis. Their eggs hatch into larvae or caterpillars. Later these become a pupa or chrysalis, within which an imago, or adult insect, develops. The larvae may live in a different habitat from the adult and require different foods.

ARE SPIDERS INSECTS?

SPIDERS belong to the class of arachnids, which also includes scorpions, ticks and mites. None of these are insects. They have eight legs, and their bodies are divided into two parts, not three.

Although they are not insects themselves, spiders are meat-eaters, feeding on insects – and other spiders.

WHICH INSECTS LIVE IN COLONIES?
·············

WASPS, bees, ants and termites live in large social groups, in which individual insects each have their part to play in the success of the whole colony. These colonies are built around a single egg-laying female, called the queen. The colonies often build large and elaborate homes. Bees make structures containing six-sided cells in which eggs and honey can be safely stored. Ants and termites often build huge mounds, with tunnels and galleries inside, to house the colony.

Honey bees are able to tell other colony members where good sources of food can be found by performing a special dance on their return to the hive.

DO INSECTS HAVE EYES?
··························

INSECTS' extraordinary compound eyes are made up of hundreds of tiny lenses. The images from all the lenses are made sense of by the insect's brain. Like us, insects can see colour, although in a different way. Flowers that seem dull to us may seem very bright to an insect. As well as having good vision, many insects have sensitive hearing and an acute sense of smell. A female moth, for example, gives off a smell that can be detected by male moths several kilometres away.

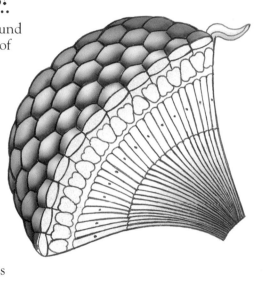

HOW DO INSECTS PROTECT THEMSELVES?
··

THERE ARE almost as many different ways in which insects protect themselves from enemies as there are different insects. Some insects, such as wasps and ants, have powerful stings or are able to shower their attackers with poisonous fluid. The hoverfly does not sting, but its colouring is so like that of a wasp or bee that enemies are very wary of it! Other insects, such as stick insects and praying mantises use camouflage. They look like the leaves and twigs among which they feed.

fast facts
·······················

WHICH IS THE BIGGEST INSECT?
···········

The goliath beetle (*Goliathus*) can weigh well over 100g (3.5oz).

ARE THERE STILL INSECTS TO BE DISCOVERED?
·····························

Well over a million species of insect are known, yet many hundreds of previously unknown insects are discovered each year.

DO INSECTS HAVE BLOOD?
······························

Insects do have blood, but it may be blue, yellow or green!

HOW CAN TINY INSECTS BE DANGEROUS TO HUMANS?
·············

Insects are very helpful to humans. While searching for food, they help to pollinate crops. By eating dead plant and animal material, they help to clean up the environment. But insects are also pests, sometimes devouring whole fields of crops in a matter of hours. They also carry diseases to plants, animals and humans. Finally, some insects have painful or deadly bites and stings.

HOW DO INSECTS HELP TO CATCH MURDERERS?
···························

Very soon after death, bodies begin to break down. This process is helped by a number of insects that feed or lay their eggs on the body. Scientists have found that these insects appear in a particular order. Examining the insects found in a body can help to pinpoint the time of death, and in many cases this has helped the police to find a killer.

The leaf katydid of Borneo is wonderfully camouflaged amongst leaves and branches. It is only when it begins to move that predators take a closer look. The burying beetle, found in the deserts of Arizona, has colouring that warns enemies that it may be poisonous.

HOW DO FISH BREATHE?

Fish are the oldest vertebrates on Earth. They are cold blooded and spend all their lives in water. They breathe by taking in oxygen dissolved in the water. Most fish breathe by using gills. They gulp in water through their mouths and pass it out through the gills, which are rich in blood and extract oxygen from the water as it passes through them.

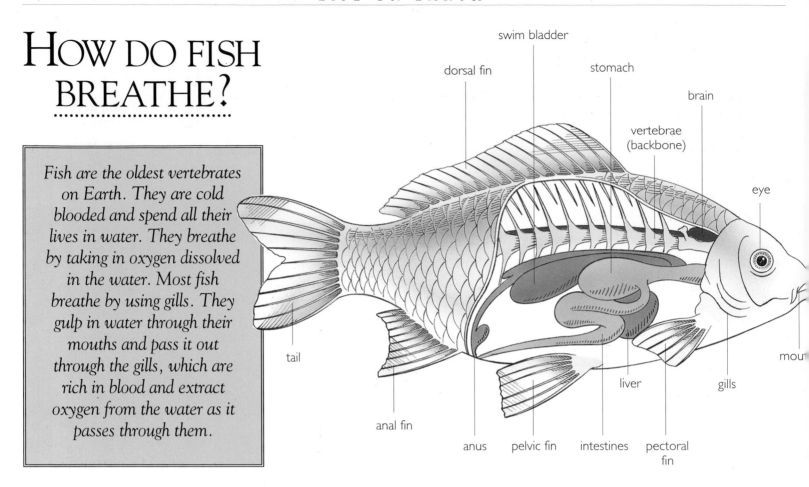

The illustration of the fish above shows features shared by all teleosts. Fish scales may be silvery or, in the tropics, glowing in bright rainbow colours.

HOW DO BONY FISH AND CARTILAGINOUS FISH DIFFER?

THE LARGEST GROUP of fish are bony fish. Most of these, making up 95% of fish species, are known as *teleosts*. They have skeletons made of bone and are usually covered with small overlapping bony plates called scales. They also have swim bladders, filled with gas, to help them remain buoyant. Cartilaginous fish include sharks, skates and rays. Their skeletons are made of flexible cartilage but, as they do not have swim bladders, they must keep moving all the time to keep their position in the water. They usually have tough, leathery skins and fleshy fins.

WHICH FISH TRAVEL THE LONGEST DISTANCES?

THE SALMON hatches in freshwater streams and rivers but then begins an incredible journey of up to 5000km (3000 miles), first to the open sea and then to return to the same river in which it was spawned in order to breed. The salmon only makes the journey once – after spawning, it dies. The European eel makes the reverse journey. It spawns in the Sargasso Sea, in the western Atlantic, and its tiny larvae swim to the shores of Europe and North America, becoming elvers (small eels) on the journey. They then spend several years in freshwater rivers and lakes before returning to the Sargasso Sea to breed. Whales also travel huge distances, this time in search of food. The tiny plankton that they eat are found more abundantly in certain areas during the year.

During its journey upstream to breed, the salmon may leap over rocks and up small waterfalls. In North America, bears wade into the river to catch some of the fish making their annual migration.

IS IT TRUE THAT MALE SEAHORSES BECOME MOTHERS?

OF COURSE, it is the female seahorse that is the real mother, producing and laying eggs. The difference is that she lays the eggs in a special pouch on the male seahorse's body. The babies develop inside the pouch and emerge when they are fully developed. As they emerge, it looks as though they are being born from the male seahorse.

It is easy to see that the seahorse was so named because of the shape of its head. In order not to be swept along by the current, the seahorse can grasp the fronds of seaweeds with its tail.

ARE ALL SHARKS DANGEROUS TO HUMANS?

ALL SHARKS are carnivorous (meat-eaters), and a few species, such as the white shark, which can grow to 9m (30ft), have been known to attack humans or even boats. But 90% of all shark species are not dangerous to humans at all.

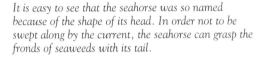

The shark's streamlined shape and muscular body enables it to move at great speed through the water. Its keen sense of smell means that it can locate and devour living or dead animals with ease. The shark's teeth are serrated, so that it can saw at the flesh of its victims.

WHAT IS A "MERMAID'S PURSE"?

A VERY FEW FISH give birth to live young, but most lay their eggs in the water, which is called spawning. A fish may lay millions of eggs, only a small proportion of which will grow into adults. A few fish, such as salmon and sticklebacks, build nests underwater to protect their eggs. They lay fewer eggs because more young survive. Dogfish and skates protect their eggs in black capsules. The empty capsules are often washed up on the beach, and it is these that are known as "mermaid's purses".

fast facts

WHICH FISH HAVE NO JAWS?

Lampreys and hagfish do not have jaws, but they do have teeth. Some of them are parasites, attaching themselves to other fish and feeding on their blood and flesh.

HOW DO SOME FISH USE ELECTRICITY?

Some fish, such as the Atlantic torpedo, the African electric catfish and the electric eel, can store electrical charges in their muscles – sometimes up to 500 volts. They may ward off attackers with electric shocks or use this extraordinary ability when catching food or attracting a mate.

WHAT IS A COELACANTH?

The coelacanth is often called a living fossil. It was known only from fossil examples until a live fish was caught off the coast of Madagascar. Coelacanths have hardly changed in the last 90 million years. They use their fins alternately, like legs, instead of together.

ARE THERE REALLY FLYING FISH?

The flying fish (*Cypselurus heterurus*) has large fins that it can spread out. When escaping its enemies, it can launch itself from the water and glide up to 100m (330ft) through the air.

HOW FAST CAN FISH SWIM?

The marlin can reach speeds of 80km/h (50mph).

WHICH IS THE SMALLEST FISH?

The dwarf goby (*Pandaka pygmaea*), which is also the smallest vertebrate, is a freshwater fish that never reaches more than 1.25cm (0.5 inches) in length.

CAN ALL AMPHIBIANS LIVE BOTH ON LAND AND IN WATER?

Amphibians have different life cycles. Many live mainly on land, but most of them spend at least some of their lives in water. Frogs, toads, newts and salamanders are all amphibians. Frogs and salamanders are able to breathe through their damp skins to a certain extent, both in the water and on land, but toads must rely largely on their lungs and cannot remain in water for long.

WHAT IS THE LIFE CYCLE OF AN AMPHIBIAN?

MOST AMPHIBIANS lay their eggs in water. Frogs' eggs are called spawn. They are protected from predators by a thick layer of jelly. Inside this a tadpole develops. When it hatches out, it is able to swim, using its long tail, and breathes through gills. As the tadpole grows, first hind legs and then fore legs begin to grow. Lungs develop, and the young frog is able to begin to breathe with its head above water. Gradually, the tail shortens until the young frog resembles its adult parents.

HOW DO FROGS AND TOADS DIFFER?

TOADS AND FROGS are similar in many ways, although toads usually have rougher, drier skins and may waddle rather than hopping as frogs do. Some toad spawn is produced in strings, like necklaces, rather than the mass of eggs laid by a frog.

Toads are often well camouflaged, easily blending into a stony or leafy background.

Adult frogs often return to the pond in which they hatched to breed.

Frog spawn hatches into larvae called tadpoles after about a week.

By 16 weeks, the froglet has four legs and almost no tail. Lungs have taken over from the gills.

By about ten weeks, the tadpole has hind legs, internal gills, and can eat small insects, worms and its smaller brothers and sisters.

At first tadpoles feed on algae and breathe through feathery gills.

HOW CAN A TREE FROG CLIMB TREES?

THE RED-EYED TREE FROG lives in the rain-forests of South America. Although it can swim, it spends much of its life out of water, among the leaves of trees where there are plentiful insects for food. The tree frog's toes have sticky pads that enable it to grip branches as it climbs.

Some tree frogs, living high in the Amazon rainforest, use the pools of water in the centre of certain tropical plants. They lay their eggs among the leaves and carry their tadpoles to water on their backs.

fast facts

WHICH IS THE LARGEST AMPHIBIAN?

The Chinese giant salamander grows up to 1.8m (6ft) long.

DO ALL AMPHIBIANS HAVE LEGS?

Caecilians are amphibians that look rather like worms. They are adapted for a life burrowing in soil or underwater. They have no legs and are practically blind, but they feel by means of tiny tentacles on their cheeks.

WHAT IS AN AXOLOTL?

Axolotls are a kind of salamander found in Mexico. Like other amphibians, they begin life as tadpoles, breathing through gills, but they never develop further and breed in the water without ever changing into an adult form.

HOW DO SOME FROGS USE A KIND OF ANTIFREEZE?

In North America, some frogs build up chemicals in their blood at the onset of cold weather. These act as a kind of antifreeze, allowing the frog to survive temperatures as low as −8°C (18°F) without freezing.

WHAT IS SPECIAL ABOUT THE MIDWIFE TOAD?

The midwife toad has a special way of hatching its eggs. The male wraps the string of eggs around its body and back legs, where they remain until they hatch.

WHAT IS THE LEGEND OF THE SALAMANDER?

IN ANCIENT TIMES, it was believed that salamanders could live in the middle of fires, as the cold of their bodies extinguished the flames around them. Of course, this is quite untrue, but the story may have come about because salamanders were often seen to run out of logs thrown onto the fire.

Salamanders and newts, unlike frogs and toads, have distinct necks and long tails in adulthood. Their bright colours warn of their poisonous skin.

HOW DO AMPHIBIANS DEFEND THEMSELVES?

AMPHIBIANS have a wide range of ways of protecting themselves. Some brightly coloured amphibians produce poisons in glands on their skins. The bright colours warn birds and animals not to attempt to eat them. Others use camouflage, blending with their surroundings, to prevent enemies from spotting them. Some frogs and toads puff themselves up or stand on tiptoes to look larger than they really are!

These frogs have skins that are coloured and speckled to blend perfectly with the background of their habitats. Camouflage is their best protection from predators.

HOW MANY DIFFERENT KINDS OF REPTILE ARE THERE?

There are four orders of reptile, by far the largest of which is the order of lizards and snakes. There are nearly 6000 different species of these. The other orders are much smaller. There are about 200 species of turtles, tortoises and terrapins, and only just over 20 species of crocodiles and alligators. Rarest of all is the tuatara, which forms an order all by itself.

WHAT ARE THE SPECIAL CHARACTERISTICS OF REPTILES?

REPTILES are cold blooded, so must gain warmth from their surroundings. This means that they can be found anywhere except in the very coldest regions of the Earth. Those that live in cooler areas usually spend the winter hibernating. Most reptiles lay eggs with hard or leathery shells. Their young hatch into miniature versions of their parents, but as reptiles can continue to grow after they are mature, some reach an enormous size.

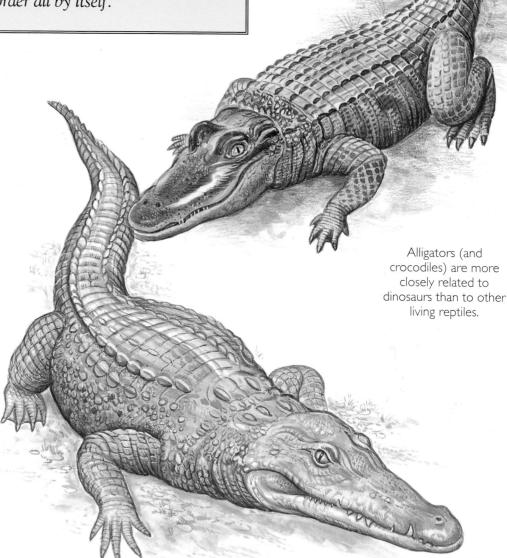

Alligators (and crocodiles) are more closely related to dinosaurs than to other living reptiles.

The giant dome-shaped tortoise of the Galapagos Islands can live to a great age and considerable size.

Crocodiles can reach up to 7m (22ft) in length.

HOW CAN YOU TELL A CROCODILE FROM AN ALLIGATOR?

BOTH CROCODILES AND ALLIGATORS spend most of their lives in swamps and rivers in warm climates, although they breathe air through nostrils on the top of their snouts, closing these off when they dive. Caymans and gavials are relatives of crocodiles and alligators. The simple way of telling them apart is that crocodiles show the fourth tooth in their lower jaw when their mouths are closed, while alligators do not. It is probably not wise to go near enough to a live crocodilian to find out, however, as they have been known to attack humans!

The sharp teeth of crocodiles and alligators enable them to grip larger prey and drag them down under the water, where they drown. They have been known to kill farm animals in this way.

HOW DOES A CHAMELEON CHANGE COLOUR?

THE CHAMELEON is able to change colour to match its surroundings by releasing or tightening special cells on its skin. As well as this remarkable ability, chameleons are amazing in other ways. They are able to grip very strongly with their toes and tails to balance on precarious branches. Their extraordinary tongues, which are able to shoot out as far as the chameleon's body length, are sticky and able to scoop back prey like a piece of elastic. Finally, the chameleon's eyes are bulging and can move in any direction, protected by an eyelid that is fused all round the eye, leaving only a tiny hole in the middle. Even stranger, the chameleon can move each of its eyes in a different direction at the same time!

Some snakes kill or immobilize their prey by injecting it with poison from their fangs. Some cobras are particularly dangerous, as they can spit their venom several feet. Other snakes squeeze their prey to death in their muscular coils.

Snakes that eat fairly large prey have flexible joints in their jaws, enabling them to open their mouths incredibly wide to swallow the prey whole.

HOW DO SNAKES MOVE?

MANY SNAKES throw themselves along the ground in waves that pass from head to tail. They have hundreds of pairs of ribs and strong muscles to enable them to do this, while their scales grip the ground. North American sidewinders, however, move as their name suggests, by throwing their coils sideways along the ground.

fast facts

WHICH IS THE LONGEST LIVING REPTILE?

The giant tortoise can live for up to 150 years.

ARE THERE ANY VEGETARIAN SNAKES?

All snakes are carnivores, eating anything from insects to small mammals.

CAN LIZARDS REALLY GROW A NEW TAIL?

If they are in serious danger from a predator, some lizards are able to discard part of their tails. The tail continues to wriggle while the lizard escapes. Within a few months, the soft part of the tail will be regrown, although it will not have bones inside it as the original tail had.

WHICH IS THE WORLD'S LARGEST SNAKE?

The anaconda and the reticulated python can both grow to over 9m (30ft) in length.

WHICH SNAKE IS THE DEADLIEST?

Up to a hundred thousand people die each year from snake bites. The snake responsible for more human deaths than any other is the Asian cobra, which is very common on the Indian subcontinent.

DO SNAKES HAVE A SENSE OF SMELL?

Strangely enough, snakes smell by using their tongues! By flicking their tongues in and out, snakes carry air to a special "smelling" gland in their mouths.

HOW DO BIRDS AND MAMMALS DIFFER?

It is likely that birds evolved from reptiles. Like reptiles but unlike most mammals, they lay eggs that hatch outside the mother. All adult birds have feathers, rather than fur or scales, and most can fly. However, birds are similar to mammals in being warm blooded.

IS IT EASY TO TELL MALE AND FEMALE BIRDS APART?

SOME MALE AND FEMALE BIRDS of the same species have very different plumage, with the male usually being more brightly coloured to attract females. Other species show little or no difference between the sexes. As well as having different plumage, birds may make displays to each other during the breeding season. Some dance in elaborate curving patterns, spread their feathers and strut, or sing. Male birds may fight to defend their territories during nesting.

The peacock displays its magnificent tail to attract the much less showy peahen. Remarkably, despite the weight of its tail feathers, a peacock can still fly.

Both male and female flamingos have pink plumage in their native habitats in Africa. They live in colonies and have long legs for wading in shallow waters.

WHAT DO BIRDS EAT?

DIFFERENT SPECIES of birds have different diets, just as mammals do. Some are vegetarian, eating fruits and seeds. Others feed on insects and other invertebrates, such as worms. Birds' beaks are adapted to the kind of food they need. The beaks of meat-eaters are often hooked and sharp, ideal for tearing flesh from carcases. Birds that search for food along the seashore or on mud banks often have long pointed beaks for burrowing into the soft ground.

A strong, short beak for cracking seeds or nuts.

A sharp, hooked beak for tearing flesh.

A long, thin beak for winkling shellfish from their shells.

A shallow, scoop-shaped beak for shovelling through mud at the bottom of ponds or estuaries.

HOW DO BIRDS FLY?

BIRDS are specially adapted for flight, whether skimming short distances between branches or flying for weeks at a time above the oceans. The shape of their wings gives a clue to the kinds of flight they make. Birds' bodies need to be light enough for flight. The large surface area of their wings pushes air downwards as they flap to lift the bird. At the same time, birds need immensely powerful chest muscles to move their wings. Feathers are the ideal covering – they are light but strong and flexible. In flight, they can lie flat against the bird's body to reduce wind resistance.

The structure of a bird's legs and wings has much in common with that of the legs and arms of humans, but they are specially adapted for flight and the bird's habitat. Swimming birds, for example, have webbed feet to help propel them through the water.

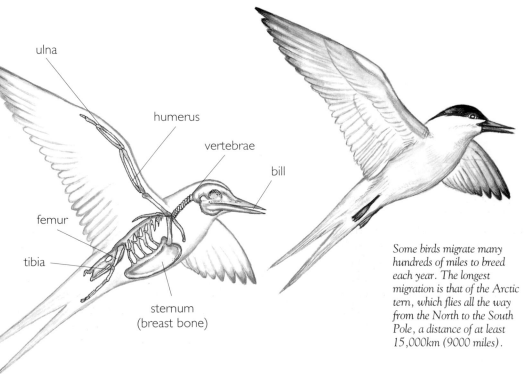

ulna

humerus

vertebrae

bill

femur

tibia

sternum
(breast bone)

Some birds migrate many hundreds of miles to breed each year. The longest migration is that of the Arctic tern, which flies all the way from the North to the South Pole, a distance of at least 15,000km (9000 miles).

WHAT ARE FLEDGLINGS?

WHEN THEY FIRST HATCH from the egg, baby birds are called nestlings. At this stage, many of them have no feathers. Blind and helpless, they are completely dependent on their parents for food and protection. As their feathers grow, they become fledglings, with open eyes and hearty appetites. When the fledglings have all their feathers and are strong enough, they are ready to learn to fly and begin to be independent.

fast facts

WHAT ARE FEATHERS MADE OF?

Feathers are made of keratin, which is a protein. Hair, hoofs and fingernails also contain keratin.

WHY ARE SOME BIRDS' BONES HOLLOW?

Hollow bones are strong but also help birds to be light enough to fly.

WHICH IS THE SMALLEST BIRD?

The bee hummingbird (*Mellisuga helenae*) is just 5.7cm (2.24 inches) long and weighs only about 1.6g (0.056oz).

HOW FAST CAN BIRDS FLY?

The white-throated spine-tail swift (*Hirundapus caudacutus*) can fly at over 170km/h (105mph).

HOW MANY FEATHERS DO BIRDS HAVE?

It varies, but some birds have more than 25,000 feathers.

WHAT KINDS OF HOMES DO BIRDS MAKE?

BIRDS show extraordinary variety and ingenuity in the nests they build. An untidy mound of sticks, simply dropped on top of one another, is all that a mute swan requires. House martins, on the other hand, literally build their homes. They skim over puddles and ponds, picking up little pieces of mud, which are built up into round-walled structures on the sides of buildings. Cuckoos, of course, are renowned for the fact that they use other birds' nests in which to lay their eggs. They are able to mimic the size, shape and colour of the host-bird's eggs to some extent, so that the additional egg is not immediately obvious.

Skilfully built, this mud nest becomes a strong structure in which several nestlings can be raised.

Dried grass, twigs, moss and feathers are easy to find for nest-building and also help to camouflage the nest.

WHICH IS THE LARGEST BIRD?

THE OSTRICH, running in herds in southern Africa, is the largest bird in the world. It can stand more than 2m (7ft) high. As well as being able to run at enormous speed from danger, the ostrich has powerful legs and sharp claws, which can deliver a kick hard enough to kill many predators.

CAN ALL BIRDS FLY?

MOST BIRDS can fly, but there are also some flightless species. These all have other ways of escaping from predators. The larger flightless birds, such as ostriches and emus, can run very fast. Penguins cannot fly but can swim and dive at great speed, using their wings as flippers to power them through the water.

WHAT IS SPECIAL ABOUT MAMMALS?

There are around 4000 species of mammal. Some spend their whole lives swimming in the ocean, while others never venture into the water. Most have fur or hair on their bodies at some time in their lives. Some walk on two legs and some on four. What all mammals have in common, however, is that they are warm blooded and breathe air. Mammal mothers feed their young on milk from their mammary glands. Mammals also have lungs, a heart with four chambers and well-developed brains.

WHY IS IT AN ADVANTAGE TO HAVE WARM BLOOD?

WARM-BLOODED ANIMALS are able to control their internal temperature to a greater degree than cold-blooded animals, so that they are less dependent on the temperature of their surroundings. While reptiles slow down when the weather is cold, mammals are able to lead an active life. Mammals have adapted to life in all parts of the world where there is food for them to eat.

Many mammals sweat or pant to lose heat if they become warm. Dogs, for example, are able to lose heat through their tongues. If the temperature becomes too cold, blood vessels contract, causing goosebumps, and muscles cause shivering in order to warm up the body with movement. Human beings, of course, can also regulate their heat by changing their clothing so that it is suitable for the conditions they meet.

WHY ARE SOME MAMMALS' BABIES ABLE TO RUN ALMOST AS SOON AS THEY ARE BORN?

ALMOST ALL MAMMAL BABIES grow inside their mother until they are able to breathe and feed outside, but mammal babies differ very much in the kind of help they need after birth. Human babies, for example, need the attention of their parents for many years before they are able to fend for themselves completely. Most grazing animals, on the other hand, have adapted to life on wide, open grasslands, where they are constantly at risk from attack by predators. It is important that these animals give birth to young that can stand on their own feet and run from danger almost immediately.

Mammal mothers produce milk for their offspring from mammary glands. The babies are able to suck the milk from nipples on their mother's stomach or chest. Usually, animals that have many babies at one time have several nipples. The mother's milk is a complete food for the babies, until they are weaned. This means introducing them to the foods they will eat as adults.

DO ALL MAMMALS GIVE BIRTH TO LIVE YOUNG?

MOST MAMMAL BABIES develop inside their mothers until they are ready to be born. The exceptions are the monotremes, a small group of mammals found in Australia. Like most reptiles, they lay eggs rather than giving birth to live young. Perhaps the best known of these is the duck-billed platypus.

Although the young of the duck-billed platypus hatch from eggs, they are mammals, so they still receive nourishment from their mother's milk. The eggs are laid underground in burrows, where the mother cares for her young until they are able to swim and forage for themselves.

WHICH MAMMAL IS THE FASTEST?

THE CHEETAH (*Acinonyx jubatus*) can reach 105km/h (65mph) when sprinting over a short distance.

WHAT IS A MARSUPIAL?

A marsupial is a very special kind of mammal. Although it does give birth to live young, they are very immature when born. Their mothers have a pouch on their abdomens, where the babies are protected and can drink milk until they are ready to survive in the open.

Female kangaroos have the extraordinary ability to keep an embryo in the womb in a state of suspended animation for several years until conditions are right for a baby (called a joey) to be born.

fast facts

WHICH IS THE LARGEST LAND MAMMAL?

The largest mammal on Earth is not a land mammal at all, but the blue whale (*Balaenoptera musculus*). The largest land mammal is the African elephant (*Loxodonta africana*), which can weigh up to 7 tonnes (6.9 tons).

CAN MAMMALS FLY?

Nowadays human beings can fly, of course, but only with the help of machines. The only mammals that can really fly are bats, which have flaps of skin between their front and hind legs, acting as wings. Other mammals, such as some possums and squirrels, can spread out their bodies and glide through the air, but they do not truly fly.

WHICH IS THE LARGEST ORDER OF MAMMALS?

There are over 1600 species of rodent, making them the largest order of mammals. Rodents have chisel-shaped front teeth, called incisors, that can be used for gnawing food. Most rodents, such as rats and mice, are quite small, but the capybara of South America can grow over a metre (3ft) long.

WHAT IS A PANGOLIN?

The pangolin is an extraordinary mammal that is covered with scales rather than fur. The pangolin eats ants, and the scales protect its body from the bites of these insects.

WHICH IS THE SMALLEST MAMMAL?

Savi's pygmy shrew (*Suncus etruscus*) weighs less than 3g (0.1oz).

WHICH ARE THE MOST NUMEROUS PRIMATES?

There are about 180 different species of primate, most of them living in the tropical regions of the world. The exception, and also the most numerous primate, is Homo sapiens – human beings. All primates have fairly large brains and forward-facing eyes that enable them to judge distances accurately. Instead of claws or hoofs, like other mammals, they have fingers and toes with soft, sensitive tips. They also have the ability to grasp with their fingers, thumbs and toes. The order of primates can be divided into prosimians, also known as primitive primates, and anthropoids, the higher primates, which include marmosets, monkeys, apes and, of course, human beings.

The ring-tailed lemur has a very long tail, like many of its relatives.

WHAT ARE PROSIMIANS?

THE PROSIMIANS include lemurs, the aye-aye, lorises and tarsiers. Lemurs live in the forests of Madagascar and nearby islands, where they eat insects, small vertebrates, shoots and leaves. They spend their time mainly in the trees, coming to the ground occasionally to feed. Most of them have long tails and many are nocturnal. Lorises come from Africa and southern Asia. They have huge, round eyes and eat insects. Tarsiers, living in the forests of Indonesia and the Philippines, also have huge eyes. Although they do not grow to more than 16cm (6.5 inches), they can leap over 1.8m (6ft) from tree to tree.

HOW DO OLD WORLD AND NEW WORLD MONKEYS DIFFER?

THE MONKEYS of the American continent, the "New" World, differ in several ways from those of Africa and Asia. New World monkeys, such as capuchins, spider monkeys, howler monkeys and woolly monkeys, have flat noses and widely spaced eyes. They live in family groups and spend much of their time in the trees, feeding mainly on fruit and leaves. Most of them have long tails, which they can use like an extra arm or leg to cling to branches. Old World monkeys live in a wide variety of habitats. They walk on all fours and, although they may sleep in trees, some species live mainly on the ground. They have narrow noses, and their nostrils face forward. Old World monkeys include macaques, mandrills and mangabeys.

The mandrill is one of the largest of the Old World monkeys. It can weigh as much as 20kg (44lb).

The cotton-top tamarin is a New World monkey, living in the forests of South America.

HOW DO PRIMATES COMMUNICATE?

PRIMATES other than humans communicate with each other in a number of ways. Many primates use touch to establish relationships, grooming each other to show friendship and to remove insects. Howler monkeys, living in the tropical forests of South America, make very loud calls. The male calls to mark his territory and can often be heard over 3km (almost 2 miles) away. Male gibbons, too, have loud calls, used for communicating with family members and to warn off other males. Some Old World monkeys have brightly coloured faces and bottoms, which the males use in courting displays and to frighten off enemies and rivals. Gorillas thump on the ground to warn off rival males, or beat their chests and roar to demonstrate their strength and power. Chimpanzees communicate with each other by using sounds and gestures.

WHICH ANIMALS ARE HUMAN BEINGS' NEAREST LIVING RELATIVES?

THE GREAT APES are the nearest living relatives to *Homo sapiens*. There are four species of great ape: the orang-utan, chimpanzee, gorilla and gibbon. Both orang-utans and gibbons spend most of their time in the trees, where they are very agile, swinging from branch to branch. Gorillas live in family groups, led by a large male, and feed mainly on the ground. The dominant male is often called a "silverback" – like humans, their hair becomes grey with age. Chimpanzees are very intelligent. They can use tools and solve puzzles. Their gestures and expressions often make them seem uncannily like humans.

All primates, including humans, take care of their young for a long time before they become adults. Apes look after their young for up to five years. Usually only one baby is born at a time.

HOW HAVE HUMAN BEINGS CHANGED THE EARTH?

There have been living things on the Earth for thousands of millions of years. It is only during the last million years that one animal has become dominant. In that time, human beings have brought huge changes to the planet, so that today there are very few places untouched by human activity. In fact, many scientists would say that our actions have had such an enormous effect that the climate of the globe has been altered, with serious consequences for every living thing that shares our Earth.

WHAT ARE THE EFFECTS OF FARMING ON THE WORLD'S WILDLIFE?

ONCE HUMAN BEINGS lived a nomadic life, hunting and gathering food as they travelled. Their lives had little effect on the ecosystems of the planet. Gradually, some nomadic peoples began to domesticate animals such as goats and sheep. By taking animals with them on their travels, they ensured a constant supply of milk, meat, skins and wool. But it was when they began to grow crops and settle in one place that humans really began to change the face of the Earth.

In huge areas of the world, natural vegetation has been ploughed up so that crops can be grown. Vast European forests were cleared for farming hundreds of years ago. Large areas of the prairies of America have been cultivated within the last two hundred years. Today the clearance still goes on as rainforests are felled. Even where land has not been ploughed, overgrazing by cattle can destroy grasslands.

Large fields without hedges can suffer from soil erosion as winds sweep across them, blowing away the topsoil.

Pesticides enter the food chain when affected insects or small animals are eaten by birds and other creatures. These in turn feed larger birds and mammals, which may be taking in harmful or even fatal amounts of chemicals.

Large fields are easier for machinery but mean that hedgerows and the habitats they provide are destroyed.

Modern intensive farming relies on chemicals to put nutrients back into the soil and kill pests. These chemicals can seep into river systems, polluting the water and damaging the habitats of many living things.

fast facts

WHY DO LIVING THINGS BECOME EXTINCT?

Living things usually become extinct because of a change in their environment. Attack by a predator, destruction of habitats or food sources and climate change can all be fatal. Humans are only a recent cause of some extinctions.

WHY IS IT IMPORTANT TO SAVE ENDANGERED SPECIES?

Living things depend on each other in complicated ways. The loss of one species may change the balance of a habitat, leading to the loss of other living things. And once a plant, for example, is extinct, it is too late to find out that it might have supplied a life-saving drug or helped to feed people or animals.

CAN THE EARTH FEED EVERYONE?

The Earth is able to produce enough food for everyone on it, but billions of people go hungry each year because they do not have access to the planet's produce.

ARE HUMANS THE BIGGEST THREAT TO LIVING THINGS?

All living things may be attacked by predators or disease, but usually a whole species is not wiped out in this way. Natural disasters, such as volcanic eruptions, fires and floods also have a local effect on wildlife. But humans can affect habitats for a long time and over a huge area.

HOW FAST IS THE WORLD'S HUMAN POPULATION GROWING?

Two hundred years ago the population of the world was around one billion (1,000,000,000). Today it is about six billion. The growth may slow in the twenty-first century, but the population is still likely to reach 10 billion before the year 2100.

WHAT IS ACID RAIN?

WHEN FOSSIL FUELS are burnt, nitrogen oxide and sulphur dioxide are given off. These substances dissolve into the moisture in the air and rise into clouds. These are blown along by the wind and fall as rain, sometimes hundreds of kilometres away. This "acid rain" kills vegetation and the living things that feed on it. It can be difficult to find the source of the problem because of its distance from the damage being done.

WHAT IS GLOBAL WARMING?

BURNING COAL AND OIL gives off carbon dioxide and other gases. At the same time, cutting down forests means that less carbon dioxide is used by plants for photosynthesis. In the modern industrial world, more and more carbon dioxide is being produced. This and other gases are known as greenhouse gases. They are held in the atmosphere of the planet and prevent heat from escaping, so warming the Earth by means of the "greenhouse effect".

CAN CITIES PROVIDE HABITATS FOR LIVING THINGS?

WHEN TOWNS AND CITIES are built, the habitats of the living things in the area are destroyed. Gradually, however, other plants and animals find a foothold in the urban environment, while a few of the original species adapt to the new conditions. Even in the largest cities there are parks, gardens and tree-lined roads. Human beings throw away an enormous amount of food, which can provide nourishment for insects, birds and animals.

At first sight a city such as New York does not appear to be an ideal habitat for wildlife, but even the largest city can provide food and homes for a wide variety of living things. Not all of these are welcomed by the city's human residents, however.

ARE WEATHER AND CLIMATE THE SAME THING?

The lower levels of the Earth's atmosphere are in constant motion. As the atmosphere heats and cools, it expands and contracts, causing changes in pressure and air movement. These changes cause the weather that we experience on Earth. The daily occurrence of sunshine, rain, hail, snow, fog or wind is what we call weather. Climate is the overall weather in a particular area over a longer period of time.

WHAT CAUSES LIGHTNING?

THE WATER DROPLETS in clouds have a positive electrical charge at the top of the cloud and a negative charge at the bottom. When the negative charge comes near enough to an attracting positive charge on the Earth below or on another cloud, the electrical energy is released in a flash of light. There may also be a loud bang, called thunder, at the same time. However, as light travels faster through the air than sound, we see the lightning flash before hearing the thunder.

WHAT IS THE WATER CYCLE?

WATER ON EARTH is constantly recycled. Water evaporates into the air from rivers, lakes and oceans. As it rises into the air, the vapour is cooled and condenses into clouds. The wind blows the clouds along until eventually precipitation – rain, snow or hail – results. The precipitation falls to Earth, where it runs through the soil to join rivers, lakes, oceans and underground reservoirs. Without water, there could be no life on Earth.

HOW DO WE DESCRIBE THE WIND?

KNOWING THE DIRECTION of the wind is not always enough. People on land and sea also need a way of describing the strength of the wind. In 1805, a British admiral called Beaufort devised the scale that still bears his name.

- **0 Calm** Smoke rises straight upwards
- **1 Light air** Smoke slowly drifts
- **2 Light breeze** Tree leaves rustle
- **3 Gentle breeze** Flags flutter
- **4 Moderate wind** Branches wave
- **5 Fresh wind** Small trees sway
- **6 Strong wind** Umbrellas misbehave!
- **7 Near gale** Large trees bend
- **8 Gale** Small branches break
- **9 Severe gale** Roof tiles dislodge
- **10 Storm** Trees blown over
- **11 Severe storm** Buildings damaged
- **12 Hurricane** Major structural damage

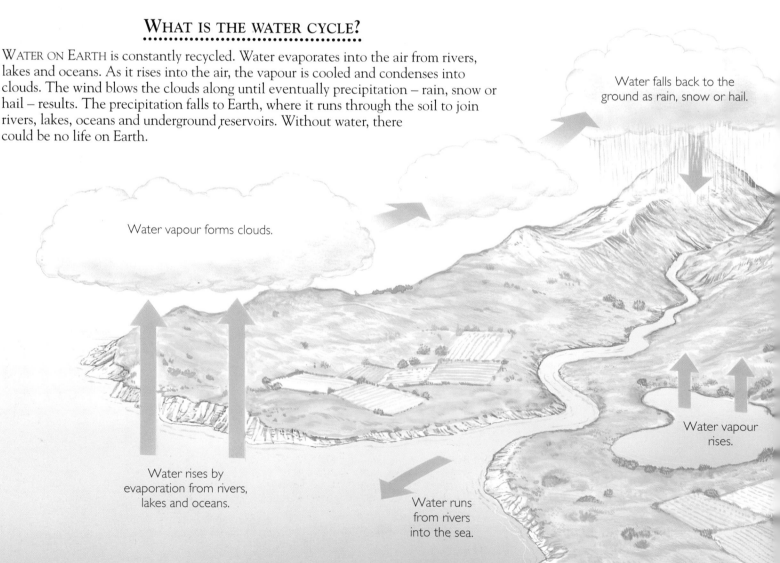

Water falls back to the ground as rain, snow or hail.

Water vapour forms clouds.

Water vapour rises.

Water rises by evaporation from rivers, lakes and oceans.

Water runs from rivers into the sea.

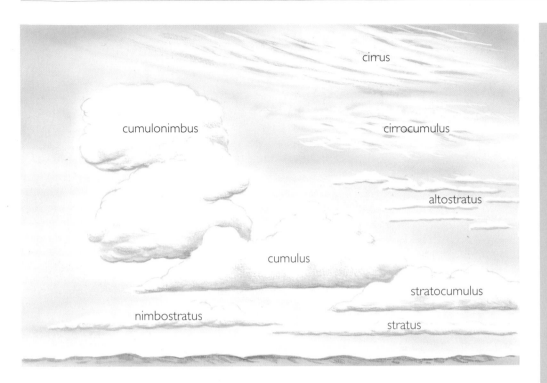

cirrus
cumulonimbus
cirrocumulus
altostratus
cumulus
stratocumulus
nimbostratus
stratus

WHAT ARE THE DIFFERENT KINDS OF CLOUD?

MOST OF THE NAMES given to different kinds of cloud simply describe their shapes and positions or give a clue about what we can expect from them. *Cirro* means "curled"; *cumulo* means "piled up"; *nimbo* means "rain"; *strato* means "in layers or sheets" and *alto* means "high". Higher levels of cloud are made of ice crystals. As you might expect, it is the clouds with the word *nimbus* or *nimbo* in their names that bring rain, hail or snow. The very lowest clouds drift over high ground as fog.

An anemometer measures wind speed.

A simple weather vane is effective for measuring wind direction.

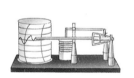

A barograph charts air pressure.

A thermometer measures air temperature.

HOW DO METEOROLOGISTS FORECAST THE WEATHER?

AS EVERYONE KNOWS, predicting the weather can often be difficult. Professional weather forecasters, called meteorologists, use information collected by weather stations on land, at sea and on satellites in space. Rainfall, sunshine and wind speed can all be measured fairly easily, but they only tell us what the weather is like *now*. A better gauge of future weather is to study air pressure and cloud formation. Today's meteorologists use computers to help make sense of all the information received and to predict, based on past events, the weather of the future.

Some people feel that age-old methods are just as effective as computers in predicting the weather. "Red sky at night, shepherd's delight, red sky in the morning, shepherd's warning" is a traditional saying.

WHICH IS THE WINDIEST PLACE IN THE WORLD?

Antarctica holds the record for being the windiest place on Earth. Although higher wind speeds have been recorded for short periods elsewhere, Port Martin regularly has winds of over 100km/h (65mph).

WHICH IS THE DRIEST PLACE IN THE WORLD?

The Atacama Desert, in Chile, is the driest place in the world. Parts of it have never had rain since records have been kept.

WHAT CAUSES THE SEASONS?

As it moves around the Sun on its yearly orbit, the Earth is slightly tilted, so that at different times of the year the northern and southern hemispheres may be slightly nearer or slightly further from the Sun. This is what causes the differences in temperature and weather that we call seasons. The equator is always about the same distance from the Sun, so its climate is the same all the year round.

WHAT IS A TORNADO?

A tornado is a wind that twists violently to form a funnel. Rising air within the funnel can literally suck objects, including buildings and people, into the air. Tornadoes are particularly dangerous because they move at high speed and can change direction very rapidly.

ARE SNOWFLAKES REALLY ALL DIFFERENT?

Examined under a microscope, all snowflakes are made up of six-sided shapes that appear to be different from each other. The problem is that no one can look at all the millions of snow crystals that form to check that there really are not two the same!

WHAT IS AN ECOSYSTEM?

Different parts of the world vary enormously in the kinds of plant and animal life they can support. This is mainly caused by the climate in each place, which allows different kinds of living things to thrive. The climate itself is influenced by the physical characteristics of a region – whether it is mountainous or near the sea, for example – and its position on the Earth – how near to the equator it is. Different parts of the world can share similar conditions, even if they are thousands of miles apart. Each area contains communities of millions of living things that rely on each other for survival. These communities are called ecosystems.

DO ECOSYSTEMS CHANGE?

OVER TIME, ecosystems can alter a great deal. The climate of the Earth has gradually changed many times even within the time when records have been kept. Before that we know that parts of the world experienced Ice Ages, which had huge effects on the environments of living things. Human beings also alter ecosystems, often without realizing the possible results of their actions. Once large areas of North America and Europe were covered with deciduous woodland. Over hundreds of years, trees have been cut down for building, to supply fuel and to clear land for farming, so that remaining areas of woodland are comparatively small.

Human beings have also altered ecosystems by introducing plants and animals from other parts of the world. European settlers in Australia, for example, took rabbits with them, which have bred in the wild and become serious pests, ousting native species.

WHERE ARE THE MAIN ECOSYSTEMS OF THE WORLD?

THE MAP BELOW shows the main ways in which the Earth can be divided into different ecosystems. These are based mainly on the kind of plants that grow in an area, as all other living things rely directly or indirectly on plants for their food. Of course, there are many smaller ecosystems within these broad divisions.

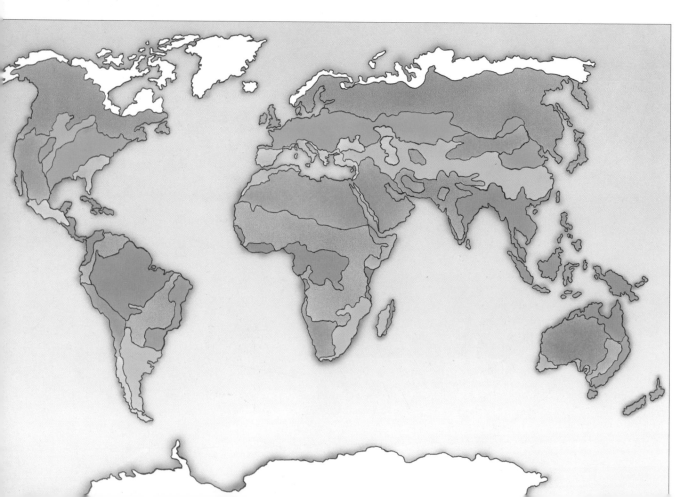

KEY

ice and tundra

coniferous forest

deciduous woodland

Mediterranean

grassland

savannah

tropical rainforest

desert

HOW DO THE MAIN ECOSYSTEMS DIFFER?

Ice and tundra
In the cold conditions of the Poles, very few species can survive, but during the summer the ice around the Arctic and Antarctic Circles melts to reveal tundra, on which sparse vegetation can live.

Coniferous forest
The coniferous forests that stretch across northern Europe, Asia and America are called the taiga. Most of the trees are evergreen, offering food and shelter to animals all the year round.

Deciduous woodland
Deciduous woodlands occur in temperate parts of the world, where the climate is fairly mild for part of the year and there is plenty of rainfall.

Mediterranean
The area around the Mediterranean Sea is known for its long, hot summers and cooler winters. Parts of Australia and North America also have this ecosystem.

Grassland
These areas are too dry to support large plants such as trees but have a variety of grasses and smaller plants on which grazing animals can feed.

Savannah
This is also grassland but it is found in tropical regions. Rainfall usually happens once a year, when grasses can grow up to 3m (10ft) tall.

Tropical rainforest
Rainforests, with their warm, moist climate, support an extraordinary variety of living things.

Desert
Desert areas have little or no rainfall. Plants and animals here have adapted to conserve every drop of available water.

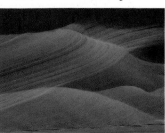

fast facts

WHAT IS A HABITAT?
Within each ecosystem there are many different places for animals to live. In the rainforest, for example, they may live high up in the tree canopy or in the rich soil below. Each place is a habitat.

HOW LARGE IS AN ECOSYSTEM?
An ecosystem can vary from an area of hundreds of square miles to a tiny pool or a single plant. A very small area may support a unique community of living things.

WHAT IS ECOLOGY?
Ecology is really the study of ecosystems – the ways in which living things live together within their surroundings.

WHY ARE THERE BATS ALL OVER THE WORLD BUT NOT ELEPHANTS?
The simple reason is that bats can fly! When the continents split from each other, different species developed on each continent, although sometimes in very similar ways.

WHAT IS THE BIOSPHERE?
The biosphere is the name given to the area on and around our planet in which life can exist.

WHICH ECOSYSTEM HAS THE GREATEST VARIETY OF LIVING THINGS?
It is likely that over half of the Earth's different kinds of living things live in the warm, moist conditions of the tropical rainforest.

DO OCEANS AND RIVERS HAVE ECOSYSTEMS TOO?
There may well be as many different ecosystems underwater as there are on land!

HOW DO LIVING THINGS SURVIVE TOGETHER?

All living things are linked in complicated food webs, relying on each other for nourishment, but some animals and plants have very special relationships, where a partnership may benefit one partner or both.

HOW DO CLOWNFISH AND SEA ANEMONES LIVE TOGETHER?

IN TROPICAL WATERS, clownfish have a symbiotic relationship with sea anemones. They live among the anemone's tentacles, unharmed by its stings but enjoying protection from predators. In turn, the clownfish seem to protect the anemone from some predators too. They may even lure fish into the anemone's tentacles, where they can be caught and digested.

WHAT IS SYMBIOSIS?

WHEN BOTH PARTNERS benefit equally from a partnership, they are said to be in a symbiotic relationship. There are many such relationships in the natural world. For example, when a bee goes to a flower to collect nectar, it also brings about pollination by carrying pollen on its furry body from one flower to the next. Both the bee and the flower benefit.

Symbiosis can sometimes help to kill parasites. Small birds called oxpeckers peck parasites from the skins of antelopes on the African savannah.

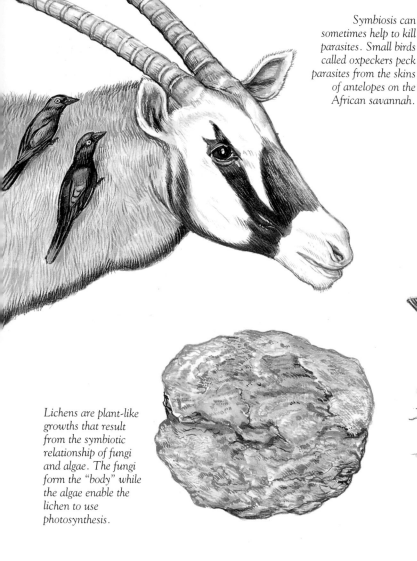

HOW DO CUCKOOS FOOL OTHER BIRDS INTO BECOMING BABYSITTERS?

CUCKOOS do not raise their own young. They are said to be brood parasites. They lay a single egg in a nest that already contains several eggs while the parent bird is away. Although cuckoo eggs are often slightly bigger than the other eggs, the female cuckoo has the extraordinary ability partially to match the colour of her egg to the others. The eggs are hatched by the host bird. The young cuckoo is bigger and stronger than the other nestlings and demands more food. To ensure that it receives all the food brought to the nest by the foster parents, it pushes the other young birds out of the nest.

Lichens are plant-like growths that result from the symbiotic relationship of fungi and algae. The fungi form the "body" while the algae enable the lichen to use photosynthesis.

WHY DO SOME DISEASES NEED ANIMAL AND HUMAN HOSTS?

EVEN THE TINIEST living things may be parasites. The micro organisms that cause malaria and sleeping sickness, for example, are parasites that need more than one host to complete their life cycles. The diseases are spread by infected insects, which bite human beings to feed on their blood and in so doing pass on the infection. The organisms multiply in the person's body, causing illness. The cycle is completed when an infection-free insect bites the person and in its turn becomes a carrier of the disease.

A parasite is a living thing that benefits from a relationship with another species but actually causes harm to that species. Some fungi are found on dying birch trees and can also live for a while on the wood after the tree has died.

HOW HAS DOMESTICATING ANIMALS HELPED HUMANS?

BY DOMESTICATING goats, cattle, sheep, pigs and poultry, humans have been able to ensure that food is always available. Horses, mules and camels have been used to carry people and goods over long distances. Pets provide companionship but can also be very useful. Sheepdogs help farmers to round up their flocks. Guide dogs for the blind and hearing dogs for the deaf help their owners to lead full lives. Animals are also used to guard property, perform rescues and carry messages.

Until the introduction of machinery, many tasks on the farm were done using the strength of horses.

Camels are used as beasts of burden in parts of the world where there are often dry conditions.

Near the Arctic Circle, dogs have traditionally been used to pull sleds. They are able to withstand the very cold conditions and move quickly over the snow.

fast facts

WHAT IS COMMENSALISM?

Commensalism is a relationship where one partner gains a benefit but the other is not affected at all.

WHICH WERE THE FIRST PETS?

Dogs were probably the first animals to be domesticated, perhaps to help with hunting. All modern dogs are related to wolves (*Canis lupus*).

WHY CAN IT BE A MISTAKE TO KILL PESTS?

A pest, such as an aphid attacking plants in the garden, may be food to an insect such as a ladybird. If all the aphids are destroyed, the ladybirds will die out too. They will then not be available to go into action if another colony of aphids arrives. Links like this between living things are happening all the time, in complicated relationships. Killing pests can affect the whole balance of an ecosystem.

ARE BACTERIA ALWAYS HARMFUL?

The human body is host to millions of bacteria. Many of these are useful, helping us to digest our food. In fact, some of the foods we eat, such as yoghurt and blue cheese, are made by allowing certain kinds of bacteria to breed in them.

WHY DO SOME ANIMALS HAVE HUNDREDS OF YOUNG AND SOME ONLY ONE?

All animals want to make sure that at least some of their young reach adulthood and reproduce themselves. Some animals do this by looking after a few babies until they can fend for themselves. Other animals produce hundreds of eggs, which they leave to develop by themselves. Most of them will die, but a few will survive, just as in smaller families.

HOW CAN GRASSLANDS SUPPORT SO MANY ANIMALS?

When not shaded by larger plants, grasses grow very quickly, especially if frequently nibbled or cut, as anyone who has to help mow a lawn knows. Up to 30% (almost a third) of the Earth's land is covered by grassland. Grass plants can survive fire, which spreads rapidly across the land but burns for only a short time, as there is little to fuel it. Flash floods are also not a problem, as the shallow, dense roots of the grasses prevent the soil from being washed away.

DO GRASSLANDS ALL OVER THE WORLD HAVE SIMILAR CLIMATES?

THE CLIMATES of the world's grasslands vary a great deal. In Africa there are huge areas of grassland called savannah. These are warm all year round with summer rains. They support large populations of seed-eating birds and grazing animals, which in turn provide food for large meat-eating animals, such as lions, leopards, cheetahs, hyenas and jackals. The North American prairies and Russian steppes are similar in having hot summers but very cold winters. Great herds of bison once roamed the North American "sea of grass", but early settlers killed enormous numbers of them for food and sport. Now the bison is a protected species. South American grasslands, called pampas, and the South African veld have sparser tussocks of grass.

Before hunting severely reduced the numbers of bison on the American prairie, it was said that a herd could take many days to pass.

WHY ARE THERE VERY FEW TREES ON VAST STRETCHES OF GRASSLAND?

IT WAS ONCE THOUGHT that large areas of grassland did not have enough rainfall or had soil that was too poor for trees to grow. Now it is also thought that they may have lost trees through fire. When grazing animals pass frequently over newly growing forest, young trees are soon killed by nibbling and trampling, so that the trees would never have a chance to become established again.

giraffe

Grant's gazelle

hyena

vulture

HOW DO GRASSES KEEP GROWING IF THEY ARE CONSTANTLY EATEN?

GRASSES are well suited to being grazed. Although many will grow to more than two metres (over six feet) if left undisturbed, they do not need to reach this height to reproduce. Even if a flower and seed head are never allowed to form, the plant can reproduce by sending out runners underground, from which new daughter plants can grow. As well as being able to grow upwards from their central stem, grasses also have lower growing points from which new stalks can grow if the central one is cut. In fact, by this means grasses grow more thickly than ever, giving more food for grazing animals to eat.

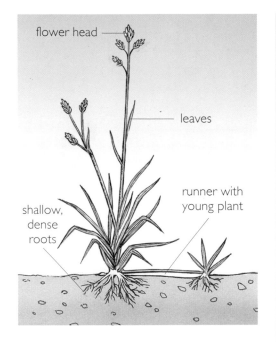

flower head

leaves

shallow, dense roots

runner with young plant

WHAT DEFENCES DO GRAZING ANIMALS HAVE AGAINST PREDATORS?

FOR MOST GRAZING ANIMALS, being part of a herd is their best defence against attack. Although individual animals, especially young, old or sick ones, may be picked off by predators, most animals will be safe. There are also more animals to watch out for danger while the rest graze. When attacked, the best defence of an antelope or zebra is its speed. At least over short distances, it can usually outrun its attackers. Wildebeest and some other heavier animals also have a powerful kick, which can break the bones of a lion or hyena if well aimed.

zebra

lion

fast facts

WHAT IS A HERBIVOROUS ANIMAL?

Herbivorous animals are plant-eaters, unlike carnivorous animals, which eat meat. Omnivorous animals, like most human beings, eat almost anything!

HOW MANY VERTEBRAE DOES A GIRAFFE HAVE?

Despite its extraordinarily long neck, a giraffe has exactly the same number of vertebrae as a human being – just 24.

DO MALE OR FEMALE LIONS HUNT FOR FOOD?

It is usually the females in a pride, or group of lions, that hunt for food.

WHAT ARE SCAVENGERS?

Scavengers are carnivores that feed on meat that is already dead. They steal meat from the kills of other animals or "clean up" when a larger animal has eaten its fill.

HOW HAVE HUMAN BEINGS CHANGED GRASSLAND WILDLIFE?

Big-game hunters have almost wiped out some kinds of grassland wildlife. Now most larger game is protected by law, but illegal poaching still goes on. In temperate areas, such as Russia and North America, large areas of natural grassland have been ploughed and used for growing crops. Although the soil is very fertile, crops often need more water and protection from the wind than grasses, which can cause problems for farmers.

ARE THERE ALSO ANIMALS LIVING UNDER GRASSLANDS?

AS GRASSLANDS usually have few trees or rocks to offer cover to smaller animals, many of them live in burrows underground. In North America, prairie dogs (*Cynomys ludovicianus*) live in huge numbers in connected burrows, sometimes causing the ground to cave in. The South American pampas also has many burrowing animals, including viscachas (*Lagostomus maximus*) and cavies (*Cavia aperea*), related to guinea pigs.

WHY ARE RAINFORESTS SO RICH IN LIVING THINGS?

Rainforests are tropical evergreen forests. They have at least 4000mm (156 inches) of rain each year. The climate is warm and moist all year round, giving conditions in which green plants can produce huge amounts of vegetation, flowers and fruit. There is always plenty to eat for insects and the animals that, in turn, feed on them. The rainforest also offers an extraordinarily wide range of habitats for living things.

WHERE ARE THE WORLD'S RAINFORESTS?

STRICTLY SPEAKING, tropical rainforests should fall within the *tropics* – between the Tropic of Capricorn and the Tropic of Cancer. In fact, most are found even nearer to the equator. South America, Africa and Asia have large areas of rainforest.

WHAT IS THE DIFFERENCE BETWEEN A LEOPARD AND A JAGUAR?

RAINFORESTS in different parts of the world often have similar species, but because they have developed separately for thousands of years, they each have their own characteristics. Both South American jaguars and African leopards have spotted skins that camouflage them in the dappled light of the forest floor. Like leopards, jaguars have rings of black spots on their coats, but they also have smaller spots within those rings.

Leopards are often nocturnal, hunting by night when lions and other predators are not active. They are also excellent climbers.

Jaguars, the largest wild cats on the American continent, prowl the forest floors of South America in search of prey.

WHY ARE RAINFORESTS IN DANGER?

RAINFORESTS are being cut down at an alarming rate for two main reasons. Both large commercial farming companies and individual families clear the forest to gain land to cultivate and graze animals, although the rainforest soil is not suitable for this use. Secondly, forests have been felled to supply tropical hardwoods for furniture-making and building. Woods such as mahogany have been highly prized in wealthy countries for hundreds of years.

ARE ALL RAINFOREST ANIMALS BRIGHTLY COLOURED?

As in most other habitats, the colouring of animals in the rainforest is very varied. Some are brilliantly coloured, to attract mates or to warn predators that they are poisonous. Other creatures have green or dark colouring to camouflage them amongst the vegetation. This hides them from their enemies and enables them to creep up on their prey unseen.

The scarlet macaw is the largest parrot in South America. Its powerful beak can crack open seeds and nuts – even Brazil nuts.

WHAT DIFFERENT HABITAT LAYERS ARE FOUND IN A RAINFOREST?

THE MANY HABITATS to be found in rainforests can be thought of as layers. In real forests, of course, these layers overlap each other a good deal.

The *emergent layer* consists of the tallest trees, with umbrella-like branches poking through the mass of leaves below. In this layer live free-flying birds and bats, including birds of prey.

The *tree canopy* consists of the leaves of mature trees. Their tops spread out to reach as much of the light as possible. As well as birds and fruit bats, monkeys and squirrels live in this layer, feeding on the fruits, nuts and leaves of the trees in the canopy.

Very little light filters through the leaves of the canopy. In the *mid-zone*, creepers called lianas hang in great ropes among the trees. Here there are monkeys, squirrels, birds and bats again, but also some snakes and tree frogs.

The *forest floor* is very dark. Larger mammals, such as deer, tapirs, elephants, jaguars and bush pigs, forage among the fallen leaves or prey on each other or smaller animals.

harpy eagle

hoatzin

spider monkey

toucan

sloth

merald ee boa

tree frog

giant armadillo

jaguar

fast facts

HOW DO PLANTS HIGH IN THE TREES GET WATER?

Some plants, called bromeliads, collect water in their cup-shaped leaves. Insects and even frogs may be found living in the tiny pool.

IS THE SOIL OF RAINFORESTS PARTICULARLY FERTILE?

The hot, moist climate of rainforests means that fallen leaves decay extremely quickly and their nutrients are taken up by the roots of plants almost at once. Nutrients are not held in the soil as happens in other environments. If the rainforest is cut down, the soil is not fertile enough for farming.

ARE SLOTHS SLOTHFUL?

Sloths are tree-dwelling mammals from South America. They hang from branches and eat leaves. It would not be fair to say that sloths are slothful, or lazy, but they do move very slowly. In fact, tiny plants called algae grow on their coats, giving them green fur!

HOW MANY SPECIES LIVE IN RAINFORESTS?

It is estimated that over two million different species of plant and animal thrive in rainforests. So far, only a small proportion of these have been discovered by humans.

WHICH RAINFOREST BIRD HAS CLAWS ON ITS WINGS?

Like many birds that live among the rainforest trees, the South American hoatzin can only fly for short distances – after all, there are too many branches in the way for long flights. Instead it climbs through the branches. Young hoatzins are helped to clamber around by tiny claws on their wings.

CAN LIVING THINGS SURVIVE WITHOUT WATER?

No plants or animals can survive if they have no water at all for a long period, but in the desert regions of the world many living things have adapted so that they can thrive with very little water. Deserts are places with very little rainfall, but they are not always hot. Some are very cold at night or in the winter. Animals and plants have to be able to deal with extreme temperatures as well as a lack of water.

HOW ARE CAMELS ADAPTED TO DESERT CONDITIONS?

CAMELS are among the largest desert animals, but they are so well adapted to dry conditions that they have been domesticated for thousands of years by people living in desert areas. They are kept mainly as beasts of burden but are also eaten and used as racing animals! Camels' feet are able to splay out to prevent them from sinking into loose sand. They are able to close their nostrils to keep out sand, and their eyes are also protected by long eyelashes. The fat in their humps is a food store. Camels very rarely sweat, so they are able to conserve the water in their bodies much more efficiently than human beings.

Camels were taken to Australia during the 1800s to enable settlers to travel across the large deserts of the interior. There are now several herds that have returned to the wild.

HOW MUCH OF THE EARTH IS DESERT?

More than a third of the Earth's land is covered by desert, but very little of it has the sandy appearance that we usually think of when deserts are mentioned. Most of the world's deserts are barren, stony places.

Like most of the world's deserts, this one in Arizona has a surface of weathered rocks, rather than sand.

Although only 15cm (6 inches) long, the jerboa has enormously strong back legs and can jump well over 2m (6ft) in one leap. Its very long tail helps it to keep its balance.

HOW DO ANIMALS SURVIVE IN THE DESERT?

IN DESERT REGIONS all over the world, animals have developed similar ways to make the best use they can of the little water that is available. Some creatures stay in burrows underground during the heat of the day, only venturing out during the night, when it is cooler. Many desert animals do not have sweat glands, and their kidneys are able to remove most of the water from their urine. Several animals have ways of storing food as fat, for use when their normal food is scarce. As well as camels, these include lizards that have fat stores in their tails.

WHAT ARE SUCCULENT PLANTS?

THE CACTI of American deserts are probably the best known examples of these plants. They store water in their fat, fleshy stems, so that they can survive in times of very little rain. Their leaves are reduced to narrow spines, so that they have a very small surface area from which to give off water by evaporation.

fast facts

WHAT IS AESTIVATION?

Aestivation is the opposite of hibernation. While some animals avoid the harsh conditions of winter by hibernating, or sleeping through the coldest months, a few desert creatures sleep underground during the hottest summer months. In other words, they aestivate!

DO DESERTS GROW?

At the moment it certainly seems as if many of the world's deserts are getting larger. This has often been caused by the actions of human beings in cutting down vegetation or over-cultivating or overgrazing the lands on the edges of deserts. Once the natural ecosystem of such an area has been destroyed, it is very difficult to repair the damage.

ARE THERE SOME ANIMALS THAT NEVER DRINK?

It seems that some desert animals do not drink at all. The kangaroo rat of North America and the jerboa of the Sahara seem to get all the moisture they need from the food they eat.

IS ALL OF THE SAHARA COVERED WITH SAND?

As well as mile after mile of sand dunes, the Sahara has rocky outcrops and several mountainous regions, where very little can survive.

ARE SOME DESERT ANIMALS POISONOUS?

In desert areas, where food for all is very scarce, animals need a quick method of killing their prey and of protecting themselves, so it is not surprising that some use poison. Among these creatures are the western diamondback rattlesnake and desert tarantula of North America and the desert scorpion of the Sahara.

The fennec fox has large ears, which allow heat to escape from its body. They are also very sensitive, allowing the fox to detect the movements of its prey.

The spiny-tailed agama is a lizard that can store fat in its tail for times when food is scarce.

WHAT CAN LIVE IN THE COLDEST PLACES ON EARTH?

As in other extreme climates, only specially adapted plants and animals can live in the coldest parts of the world. In fact, at the North and South Poles, almost nothing can survive, but around the edges of the Arctic and Antarctic there are seas rich in plant and animal life. This means that larger animals, living on the edge of the ice, can find food in the teeming waters.

HOW DO THE ARCTIC AND ANTARCTIC DIFFER?

AT THE North and South Poles there are areas that are covered by thick layers of snow and ice all year round, but the two areas are very different. The Antarctic region, around the South Pole, has land far under the ice. The Arctic region, around the North Pole, is actually frozen sea. It is possible for a submarine to travel right under the North Pole. Because in polar regions the sea is warmer than the land or ice, the Arctic, with more sea, is not as cold as the Antarctic.

DO THE POLAR REGIONS HAVE SEASONS?

THERE ARE SEASONAL VARIATIONS at the Poles, but these are much more noticeable in the Arctic than in the Antarctic. During the Arctic summer the sea ice begins to melt and break away in large icebergs. Although the area around the North Pole is always covered by ice, the snow melts around the edges of the Arctic Circle so that Arctic animals can browse on the sparse vegetation. One result of this is that some Arctic mammals, who need camouflage to keep them safe from predators, change the colour of their coats from white in the winter to brown in the summer months.

Arctic hares turn white in the winter. In summer they moult to reveal brown coats that camouflage them against the tundra.

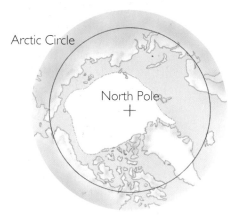

THE ARCTIC

Arctic Circle

North Pole
+

ANTARCTICA

Antarctic Circle

South Pole
+

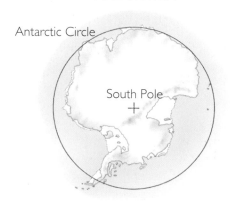

HOW DO POLAR ANIMALS KEEP WARM?

IN VERY COLD CLIMATES, animals need excellent insulation to stop their body heat from escaping. This may be on the outside, in the form of dense hair, fur or feathers, or on the inside, in the form of a thick layer of fat or blubber.

Many kinds of seal live in the Arctic Ocean, feeding on fish and shellfish. They come out of the water to give birth to their pups.

HOW DO PENGUINS KEEP THEIR EGGS WARM?

PENGUINS are only found in the southern hemisphere, not in the Arctic. Many penguins lay only one egg during the dark days of winter. One penguin "sits" on the egg, holding it off the ice with its feet, until it hatches two months later.

The macaroni penguin huddles over its egg, keeping it warm and protecting it from predators.

HOW DOES THE WALRUS USE ITS TUSKS?

DURING THE BREEDING SEASON, walruses gather on the Arctic ice. The males fight each other for the females, often causing serious wounds with their long tusks. But the main reason for these impressive extended teeth is for digging up shellfish from the ocean floor.

Polar bears are fierce predators. They wait by holes in the ice to catch seals that come up for air. Although they are large, polar bears are very fast and excellent swimmers.

No one is quite sure why the narwhal has such a long tusk. It is a mammal, giving birth to live young underwater.

fast facts

WHERE IS THE COLDEST PLACE ON EARTH?

The average temperature at the South Pole is around –50°C (–58°F), although temperatures 40°C (104°F)✓ lower have been recorded.

WHAT IS THE ARCTIC UNICORN?

Some people believe that stories of unicorns came about because sailors found the horns of narwhals and did not know that they came from a sea mammal.

WHICH IS THE LARGEST POLAR MAMMAL?

Although polar bears in the Arctic are very large, the biggest polar mammal does not live on land at all. It is the blue whale, which swims around the Antarctic Circle and is the largest mammal ever to have lived on Earth. Despite its huge size, the blue whale survives by eating tiny shrimp-like creatures called krill (*Euphausia superba*).

HOW DO POLAR BEARS AVOID SLIPPING ON THE ICE?

Polar bears have very hairy feet! These help them to grip the ice, and their sharp claws enable them to take a firmer grip still.

WHAT IS TUNDRA?

Tundra is the name given to the bleak land of the Arctic that is only covered by ice and snow in the winter. During the summer, many species of plant grow there, but the earth is too cold for their roots to reach down far. Grazing animals, such as reindeer and the musk ox, feed on the low-growing plants.

The Arctic Ocean is rich in fish, shellfish and krill, which are tiny shrimp-like animals. These in turn feed on microscopic plant life.

IS THERE LIFE IN THE DEEPEST OCEANS?

It is likely that life on our planet began in the oceans. As much more of the Earth is covered with water than with land, and the sea can be thousands of metres deep, there is simply more space for living things in the oceans. However, the conditions that they experience there are not so varied, so there are fewer different species than there are on land. Well over 90% of the living things that thrive in the oceans are found in the fairly shallow waters around the continents. However, scientists have found that there is life even in the deepest oceans, although it is not easy to study wildlife in such remote areas.

WHAT IS A CONTINENTAL SHELF?

AROUND THE CONTINENTS of the world there are areas of fairly shallow sea called continental shelves. Here the sea bed is quite flat and only about 130m (430ft) below the surface. There is usually plenty of marine life in these areas. Beyond the shelf, the sea floor drops, so that the sea is much deeper further from shore. In the middle of the oceans, however, the sea bed rises into a ridge, where the plates of the Earth's crust meet.

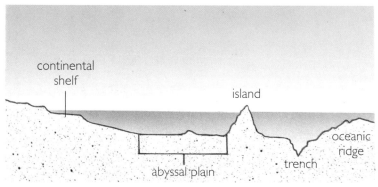

Most commercial fishing takes place in the waters above continental shelves. The deepest ocean is found in trenches where the sea floor plunges hundreds of metres.

HOW DO OYSTERS MAKE PEARLS?

PEARL OYSTERS are molluscs. Their soft bodies are protected by a tough outer shell, hinged at one side. When a piece of grit becomes embedded in the soft body of the oyster, it protects itself by building up layers of a shiny, shell-like material around the foreign body. This happens naturally, but today many pearls are cultivated in oyster farms, where "seeds" are injected into the oysters so that they will form pearls.

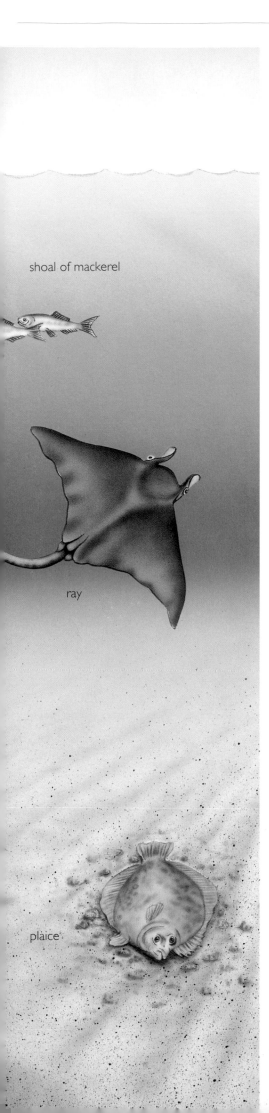

shoal of mackerel

ray

plaice

HOW DO SCIENTISTS INVESTIGATE OCEAN LIFE?

BY CARRYING OXYGEN TANKS, divers can examine the wildlife of the top few metres of the oceans, but for deeper investigations, where the water pressure is higher, they need diving suits or specially adapted submersibles. Mechanical arms can be operated from within the sub to retrieve samples of plants, animals and minerals.

Fortunately, most ocean life is within reach of divers carrying oxygen. Coral reefs are particularly rich in living things.

WHY DO SOME FISH HAVE BOTH EYES ON THE SAME SIDE?

WHILE MANY FISH swim in shoals, eating plankton as they flash through the water, others spend most of their time on the ocean bed. As the fish evolved, their eyes developed on the same side, so that both can see into the water above.

Some fish use camouflage just as land animals do. While they are not moving, it can be very difficult to see them among the sand and stones of the sea bed.

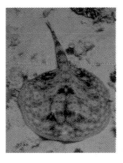

fast facts

HOW MUCH OF THE EARTH'S SURFACE IS COVERED BY SEA?

Over two-thirds (71%) of the Earth's surface is covered by the oceans.

WHAT IS PLANKTON?

Plankton is the millions of tiny plants and animals, too small to see without a microscope, that live in huge numbers in the oceans. They are food for many species, including some of the largest ones – whales.

WHY IS THE SEA SALTY?

The sea is salty because chemicals from rocks and soil have been dissolved in it. These include sodium, chlorine (which together make the salt we put on our food), magnesium, calcium and potassium.

HOW DEEP IS THE DEEPEST OCEAN?

The deepest ocean known is in the western Pacific. It is called the Marianas Trench and is about 11,000m (36,000ft) deep. Mount Everest could be placed in it and there would still be thousands of metres of water above it.

WHICH IS THE FURTHEST MAMMAL MIGRATION?

The longest mammal migration takes place in the oceans. The blue whale travels up to 20,000km (12,500 miles) each year.

CAN DEEP-SEA CREATURES SEE IN THE DARK?

OCEANS offer various habitats at different depths below the surface. These are called zones. The euphotic zone is at the top, ending at a depth of about 200m (660ft). Below this, very little light from the Sun can reach. The bathypelagic zone below is totally dark, so no plants can live there, but a number of fish, squid and crustaceans do make this zone their home, feeding on waste material that sinks down from above and on each other. Deep-sea creatures cannot see in total darkness, but their other senses help them to find food. Some, such as angler fish, carry their own lights. They are not bright enough to search for food by, but they may lure other fish towards them and help fish of the same species to recognize each other.

HOW DO FRESHWATER ECOSYSTEMS OPERATE?

Freshwater habitats include both still and moving water. Living things within rivers and streams can travel through the water to different areas. Many underwater inhabitants of ponds and lakes, however, cannot escape from what may be quite a small area of water. However, even a tiny pool may have a complete, self-contained ecosystem. As well as plants and fish, freshwater ecosystems support living things that visit the water but spend part of their lives on land, such as amphibians, birds and insects. Many mammals also spend time in and around the water. Finally, the kinds of wildlife found in freshwater ecosystems will be affected by the climate and landscape around it. For example, the crocodile may be the fiercest predator in an African river, but its place may be taken by an otter in a European stream.

The wildlife to be found in fresh water varies a great deal, depending on whether the water is still or moving and on the climate of the surrounding countryside. In the Brazilian rainforest, the Amazon is as teeming with life as the forest itself. The giant water lily is the largest in the world. The leaves are strong enough to support a small child!

WHERE DOES THE WATER IN PONDS AND RIVERS COME FROM?

PONDS AND RIVERS are part of the water cycle – the water that is constantly evaporating from the Earth, forming clouds and coming back to Earth as rain or snow. Some of this water seeps into underground streams and pools, which in turn may feed a spring that is the source of a river. Other rivers are fed by melting glaciers or very large lakes.

Although many parts of the world appear to have plenty of surface fresh water, in fact most of the world's fresh water is held underground or as ice. Less than 0.5% is to be found in rivers, lakes and the atmosphere.

DO FISH BUILD HOMES?

ALTHOUGH they often lay hundreds or even thousands of eggs, some fish do build nests to protect their young. The stickleback, found in European ponds and rivers, builds a nest of plant fibres in which the male guards the eggs until they have hatched, chasing away even the female that laid them.

dragonfly

newt

HOW IS AN OXBOW LAKE FORMED?

AS A RIVER FLOWS through countryside, it rarely follows a straight line, but bends and twists following the natural contours of the ground and washing away the softest soil. Water flows fastest on the outer side of the bends, causing that bank to wash away further. In the meantime, soil being carried along in the river water, called silt, is deposited on the opposite bank. Over time, especially if there is flooding, the river may cut across the neck of the bend, creating an oxbow lake beside the river.

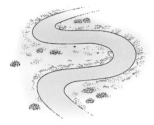

The river meanders as it crosses flat ground.

The river's current causes the bend to become greater and silt to be deposited on the bank opposite.

The river breaks through the neck of the bend and leaves an oxbow lake to one side.

WHY DO BEAVERS BUILD DAMS?

BEAVERS are rodents with very long, sharp front teeth. They use their teeth to gnaw down small trees for use in dam building or for food. Beavers build dams of sticks and mud across a river. This makes a calm pool the other side of the dam in which the beaver can build its home, or lodge. The inside of the lodge is reached by means of underwater tunnels. This keeps the beaver safe from predators such as wolves, even when the surface of the water is frozen in winter.

The beaver's thick fur keeps it warm in wet and icy conditions. In the past it also attracted fur trappers.

moorhen

stickleback

great diving beetle

HOW DOES WATER FLOW EFFECT FRESHWATER WILDLIFE?

A FAST-FLOWING RIVER sweeps soil from the riverbed so that plants cannot grow there. On the other hand, there is more oxygen dissolved in the water, so that fish such as salmon thrive. Rivers in areas where the soil is peaty often have very little wildlife, because acid from the soil washes into the water.

WHAT ARE LIVING THINGS MADE OF?

Everything in the universe is made of atoms, arranged in different ways. But living things, unlike rocks or metal, have larger building blocks called cells. Some living things have only one cell, while others contain millions. Each cell has a job to do, but they all work together to make a living organism.

WHAT IS A CELL?

CELLS certainly are the building blocks of life, but they are very busy building blocks! Inside each cell thousands of chemical reactions are going on, so that the cell can carry out its tasks. A typical cell has a cell wall or membrane surrounding a kind of watery jelly called cytoplasm. Within the cell there are a number of parts called organelles. These do all the work that the cell is designed to do. The nucleus is a particularly important organelle. It controls all the activities of the cell.

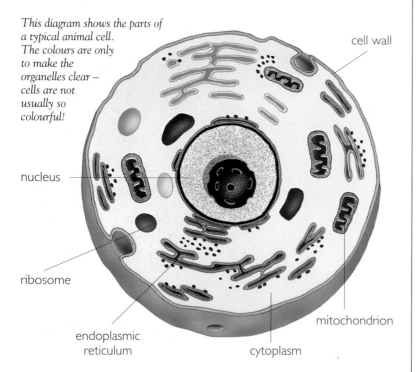

This diagram shows the parts of a typical animal cell. The colours are only to make the organelles clear – cells are not usually so colourful!

cell wall

nucleus

ribosome

endoplasmic reticulum

cytoplasm

mitochondrion

WHAT ARE MITOCHONDRIA?

MITOCHONDRIA are organelles that break up food materials to make energy. Other important organelles are ribosomes, which make proteins, and endoplasmic reticulum. This is a structure, made of double membranes, that is linked to the nucleus and to the cell wall, so that chemicals can be carried around the cell. The cell wall itself is said to be semi-permeable. That means that some chemicals can pass through it into the cell but none can pass out.

WHAT DO ALL LIVING THINGS HAVE IN COMMON?

LIVING THINGS are said to be animate. Inanimate things are not living. Metal, plastic and glass, for example, are inanimate. All animate things are able to do six things that inanimate things cannot.

1. They can feed, taking in nutrients that can be used for energy or to build or renew body parts.

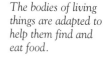

The bodies of living things are adapted to help them find and eat food.

2. They can grow. They may stay the same shape and simply become larger, or they may take on various forms during their life cycle.

Living things may grow to enormous size over hundreds of years.

3. They can respire, taking in gases from the air and using them as part of the process of converting food into energy.

Fish respire by taking in oxygen dissolved in the water through their gills.

4. They can excrete, getting rid of waste material through their surfaces or by means of special parts of the organism.

Some animals, such as rhinos, use excretions to mark their territory.

5. They are sensitive, reacting to stimuli from outside.

Horses can be trained to respond to the most delicate touch of a rider.

6. They can reproduce, creating new versions of themselves in order that the species will not die out.

Most larger mammals produce only one or two offspring at a time.

All animals and many plants are also able to move. Plants cannot move their whole bodies in search of food, shelter or a mate, as most animals can, but many can move in a very small way, bending towards light, for example.

HOW DO PLANT CELLS DIFFER FROM ANIMAL CELLS?

ALL CELLS have a cell wall, but in plant cells this is made of a stiff, tough layer of cellulose. Cellulose is made of tiny fibres, layered together to form a strong sheet. Most plant cells also contain organelles called chloroplasts. It is in these that photosynthesis takes place.

Plants do not have skeletons to form a rigid framework for their bodies. Instead, stiff cell walls hold them up.

WHAT IS DNA?

DNA IS AN ABBREVIATION of the name of a chemical: deoxyribonucleic acid. It is DNA that contains the instructions for making and controlling every living thing. Inside the nucleus of a cell, the DNA forms chromosomes. Living things have different numbers of chromosomes. Human beings have 46, arranged in 23 pairs. Each of us has inherited one half of each chromosome pair from our father and the other half from our mother. A gene is a small part of the DNA molecule that can make one of the proteins that the living organism needs.

The molecules of DNA are in the form of a spiral, making a shape called a double helix.

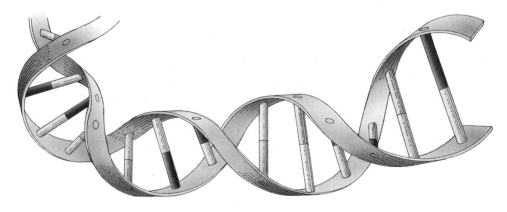

HOW DO LIVING THINGS GROW AND AGE?

Two things affect the way in which living things grow and age. The first is their genetic make-up – the genes that they have inherited from their parents. The DNA in their chromosomes controls the way that cells divide to cause the growth of the young organism, its coming to maturity and its aging. The other important factor is the environment and conditions that the organism experiences – how much of the right kind of food it eats, where it lives, the climate and the kinds of events and accidents that happen to it.

WHAT ARE THE LONGEST ANIMAL LIFE SPANS?

HUMAN BEINGS are far from being the longest-living animals. The giant tortoise can reach 150 years, while several aquatic creatures, such as the killer whale and some species of sea anemone, can survive for well over 80 years. At the other end of the scale, the adult mayfly lives for less than two days. The plant kingdom has far longer-living species. Several trees, such as the yew and giant sequoia, live for thousands of years.

WHAT IS GESTATION?

GESTATION is the length of time between conception – the fertilization of an egg by a sperm – and the birth of the baby that grows from the fertilized egg. The length of gestation varies according to the species.

Asian elephant : 660 days

cow: 278 days

human being: 267 days

cat: 61 days

dog: 63 days

mouse: 20 days

These are average gestation periods. The birth can be several days earlier or later than the average.

HOW ARE CHARACTERISTICS PASSED FROM ONE GENERATION TO THE NEXT?

THE CHARACTERISTICS of individual human beings are passed from one generation to the next in their chromosomes. Each of our parents gives us 23 chromosomes, making 46 in all. That means that we have two versions of each of our genes, but one is often dominant. We see the effect of the dominant gene, but the other (recessive) gene is still there and can be passed to our children.

Bb   Bb

BB   Bb   Bb   bb

*In this diagram, **B** stands for brown eyes and **b** stands for blue eyes. If a child inherits one brown-eyes gene and one blue-eyes gene, she will have brown eyes, but she still has a blue-eyes gene to pass on to half of her own children. If her children's father also has brown eyes but a recessive blue-eyes gene, on average one in four of her children will inherit two blue-eyes genes and therefore have blue eyes.*

Our genes are inherited from our parents, which is why resemblances between family members can often be seen.

HOW DO HUMAN BABIES DEVELOP?

Human beings are mammals, which means that their young develop inside the mother until they are ready to be born. This development takes place inside the womb or uterus, where the baby gains the nutrients and oxygen it needs for growth from its mother's own blood, supplied through the umbilical cord.

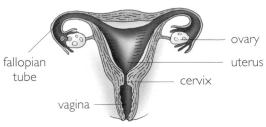

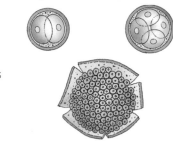

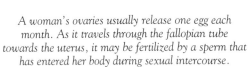

A woman's ovaries usually release one egg each month. As it travels through the fallopian tube towards the uterus, it may be fertilized by a sperm that has entered her body during sexual intercourse.

As soon as it is fertilized, the egg cell begins to divide, until it becomes a ball of cells called a blastocyst. This ball then implants itself in the wall of the uterus.

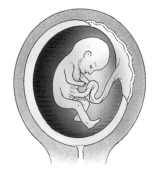

After four weeks, the blastocyst has become an embryo. Its brain, spine and limbs are already forming and its heart will soon begin to beat.

At 12 weeks, the embryo is now called a foetus. All its organs are formed. For the rest of the time before it is born, it simply has to grow.

From 38 weeks onwards, the baby is ready to be born. It moves down into the pelvis. At birth, the cervix gradually opens and the baby is born through the vagina.

Although human babies are quite helpless at birth, by nine months most are on the move by crawling or sliding along, and within a year they will be able to eat solid food, walk and begin to understand language.

HOW MUCH LONGER ARE PEOPLE LIVING NOW THAN IN THE PAST?

In many parts of the world, life expectancy – the number of years that a person can expect to live – is increasing. A thousand years ago, 40 might have seemed a good age for an adult to reach. Now we expect to live twice as long. Of course, these are just averages. Since records began there have been exceptional people who lived to 80 and beyond, but for most people, the dangers of dying of disease, accident, war or starvation were very high. Childhood in particular was a dangerous time. A woman might give birth to more than 10 children, none of them living to adulthood. We must not forget that there are parts of the world where this is still true, and billions of people still die each year from lack of food or medical care.

HAVE ALL HUMAN POPULATIONS INCREASING NUMBERS OF OLDER PEOPLE?

In the developed world, populations are aging, as better health care means that more people are living longer, while younger people are having fewer children. But in developing countries, where recent improvements in medical attention mean that fewer babies die in their early years, there are far more young people, under the age of 20, in the population than any other group.

WHY DOES SKIN WRINKLE WITH AGE?

As we get older, our skin becomes less elastic. We also tend to become thinner, so there is less fat beneath the skin to plump it out.

WHY CAN'T PEOPLE LIVE FOR EVER?

Every living thing has a natural lifespan. Gradually, the parts of the body do not repair and maintain themselves so effectively and most processes become weaker, until one breaks down and the organism dies. However, as scientists learn more about aging, it may be that the human lifespan can be lengthened.

DO HUMAN BEINGS SHED THEIR SKIN?

Human beings shed tiny particles of skin all the time. In fact, a large proportion of house dust is made up of human skin!

DO PEOPLE REALLY BECOME SHORTER AS THEY AGE?

In old age, our muscles weaken and there is a tendency to stoop, making us look shorter. In addition, the cartilage between the bones of our spine becomes thinner, reducing our height.

WILL LIFE ON EARTH GO ON FOR EVER?

Life on Earth cannot go on for ever because it depends on the Sun and, like all stars, our Sun will eventually die. However, that will happen billions of years in the future. In the meantime, we need to be concerned about the way in which we are using our planet now, so that it will continue to provide a home for all the living things that share it with us in the next century and beyond.

WHAT ARE NON-RENEWABLE RESOURCES?

LIVING THINGS can grow and reproduce themselves. Given the right conditions, they can continue to do this for millions of years. But some of the Earth's resources cannot renew themselves. When they have been used up, there will be no more. Perhaps the most important of these non-renewable resources are what are known as fossil fuels. Both oil and coal were made millions of years ago when the bodies of prehistoric plants and animals were crushed under enormous pressure beneath moving rock. There is a limited supply of these fuels, making it necessary for us to develop energy sources that cannot run out.

WHICH KINDS OF ENERGY WILL NOT RUN OUT?

WIND, moving water and sunshine are always to be found somewhere on the Earth. All of these can be harnessed to provide energy. Wind farms, consisting of fields of enormous windmills, have been set up in many parts of the world to capture the wind's energy. Hydroelectric power uses the force of water hurtling over dams. Solar panels are warmed by the Sun and can be used to heat water and homes. At the moment, these methods are not able to produce all the energy that the world needs, but they hold out hope for the future.

Pylons carrying electricity cables are such a familiar sight that it is hard to remember that two hundred years ago no one had any electrical appliances, lighting or heating.

Wood is a renewable resource as new trees can be planted, but it is not suitable for use as fuel on a large scale. After all, it takes only a few hours to burn a tree trunk but thirty years to grow another one.

wind farm

hydroelectric power station

solar panels

DOES THE PLANET HAVE ITS OWN RECYCLING SYSTEMS?

THE SAYING that there is nothing new under the Sun is strangely true. The stuff that makes up everything on Earth – animals, plants, rocks, water – cannot be destroyed, although it can be changed from one form to another. Living things are almost entirely made up of six elements: carbon, oxygen, hydrogen, nitrogen, phosphorous and sulphur. When a plant or animal dies, it decomposes. Gradually, its body breaks down, and the elements it was made of go back into the soil or water. These elements in time are taken up by new plants, which in turn are eaten by animals. This cycle of elements being released and re-used can take millions of years, but it is quite likely that within your body there are chemicals that were once part of a prehistoric plant – or even a dinosaur!

WHAT ARE THE MAIN PROBLEMS OF SPACE TRAVEL?

THE BIGGEST PROBLEMS of space travel all have to do with the enormous distances that are involved. Using today's technology, it would take years to reach even the nearest planets, and generations of space travellers would live and die on a journey to more distant ones. For this to happen, spacecraft will need to be self-supporting or able to travel faster than the speed of light.

COULD HUMANS FIND HOMES ELSEWHERE IN THE UNIVERSE?

AS THERE ARE BILLIONS of planets in our universe, it is likely that some of them could support life, but the vast distances that would have to be travelled to reach them are at present an immense problem. More possible is the idea that humans could build self-supporting communities on nearby planets. Ideally, these would need to be enclosed, containing their own atmosphere and able to support a variety of plant and animal life just as our planet does. Experiments are being made to see if it is possible to build artificial ecosystems like this here on Earth.

The Moon is so near that it would be possible to take day trips there! But it has no oxygen, so no living thing could survive there except inside a specially constructed building or suit.

COULD SCIENCE FICTION STORIES EVER COME TRUE?

SCIENCE FICTION STORIES do come true all the time. Less than a hundred years ago, space travel was a fantasy invented by storytellers such as H G Wells and Jules Verne. When we consider the extraordinary advances made in the fields of travel and communications in the past century, it is tempting to believe that *Star Trek* may in the future be nearer to reality than at present seems possible!

By studying the way in which the Earth's natural systems renew themselves, scientists hope to learn how to create successful ecosystems on other planets.

fast facts

HOW CAN HUMANS HELP WITH RECYCLING?

The first step is not to use too many of the Earth's resources in the first place. For example, we can try to use less fuel and buy fewer products that have a great deal of packaging. Many items that we need to use, however, can be recycled. Glass, paper, metals, plastics and even textiles can be recycled. Centres have been set up in many areas where household waste of this kind can be taken for recycling.

CAN OUR PLANET KEEP ITSELF IN BALANCE?

Some people believe that our planet is wiser than the people that live on it. They reason that life has continued on Earth for billions of years, despite natural "disasters" such as Ice Ages. The whole Earth (and the living things on it) is itself like a living organism, constantly adapting to the conditions in which it finds itself. This is a comforting thought, but it is wise to remember that we need the Earth much more than the Earth needs us. After all, life on Earth developed for millions of years before humans evolved.

HOW CAN POLLUTION BE REDUCED?

Pollution is the name we give to waste products that enter the air and soil and water but cannot be quickly broken down by natural processes. Instead, they affect the health of plants and animals, including humans, and the environments they live in. Controlling the emissions of factories and vehicles can help. It is also important, as far as possible, to use materials that can break down in the soil when they are thrown away. Such materials are said to be biodegradable.

GLOSSARY

Antifreeze   A substance added to a liquid to raise the temperature at which it will freeze. Antifreeze added to the water in a car's radiator will prevent it from freezing except at very low temperatures.

Atmosphere   The gases that form a layer around a planet.

Botanist   A scientist who studies plants.

Camouflage   The way in which the shape, colour or markings of a living thing can help it to blend into its surroundings and protect it from notice by its enemies.

Carnivorous   Meat-eating. An animal that eats both plants and animals is said to be omnivorous.

Classification   Organizing items into different classes or divisions. This helps scientists to describe them properly and to observe similarities and differences between them.

Condensation   The changing of a gas or vapour into a liquid, often the result of cooling the gas or vapour.

Constellation   Stars that appear to form a group or pattern when viewed from Earth.

Continent   A very large body of land, surrounded by sea.

Environment   The surroundings of a living thing.

Evaporation   Molecules of a liquid escaping into the atmosphere to form vapour.

Hibernation   Sleeping or greatly slowing down the body's functions during the winter.

Hominid   A member of the primate family that walks on two legs, as people do.

Horticulturist   A person concerned with growing and breeding plants, especially for gardens.

Life cycle   The stages that a living thing normally goes through during its lifetime.

Metamorphosis   Literally, changing form. The word is often used of the changing of a larva to a pupa in the insect world.

Nomad   A person with no settled home, who moves about in search of food and shelter, often following the migrations of animals throughout the year.

Nutrient   Something that gives nourishment. Part of the food of a living organism.

Orbit   The path that a body takes as it circles another body, especially a planet or moon circling a star.

Organism   A living thing, such as a plant or animal. Living things are made up of one or more cells.

Planet   A large heavenly body that is in orbit around a star. A smaller body that is in orbit around a planet is called a moon.

Plankton   Microscopic plants and animals that live near the surface of the sea and provide food for many sea creatures.

Predator   An animal that hunts other animals for food.

Reproduction   The creation of a new living thing similar to its parents. Sexual reproduction requires a male and female parent, while asexual reproduction can be achieved by a single organism.

Satellite   Something that orbits a planet. This may be an artificial satellite, put into orbit by scientists, or a natural satellite, such as a moon.

Segment   A section of the body of a plant or animal marked off by a clear line or division. Often such an organism has several similar segments making up its body.

Serrated   With a saw-like edge.

Stimulus   Something that prompts an organism or part of an organism into action or response.

Vegetation   Plants of all kinds, especially those with abundant or large leaves.

INDEX